READING
JOURNAL

This Journal Belongs To:

_____

Journal Timeline:

_____

REVIVE *stationery*

Reading Journal

ISBN: 978-1-83412-028-7

INDEX

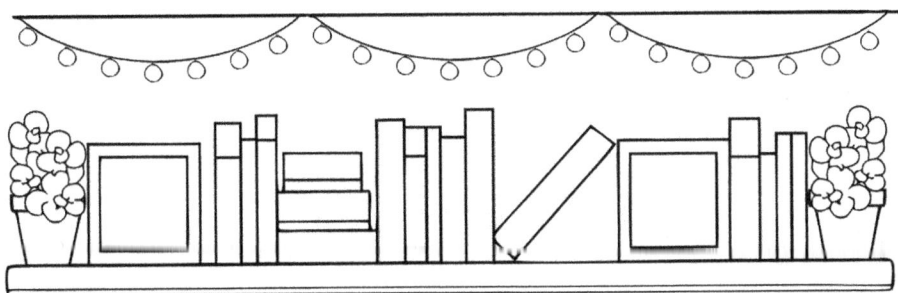

BOOK LOG

BOOK LOG

BOOK LOG
KEEP TRACK OF YOUR BOOKS IN ONE PLACE!

#	TITLE	AUTHOR	SERIES?	RECOMMEND?	ABANDONNED?	RATING (1-5)
			☐	☐	☐	☆☆☆☆☆
			☐	☐	☐	☆☆☆☆☆
			☐	☐	☐	☆☆☆☆☆
			☐	☐	☐	☆☆☆☆☆
			☐	☐	☐	☆☆☆☆☆
			☐	☐	☐	☆☆☆☆☆
			☐	☐	☐	☆☆☆☆☆
			☐	☐	☐	☆☆☆☆☆
			☐	☐	☐	☆☆☆☆☆
			☐	☐	☐	☆☆☆☆☆
			☐	☐	☐	☆☆☆☆☆
			☐	☐	☐	☆☆☆☆☆
			☐	☐	☐	☆☆☆☆☆
			☐	☐	☐	☆☆☆☆☆
			☐	☐	☐	☆☆☆☆☆
			☐	☐	☐	☆☆☆☆☆
			☐	☐	☐	☆☆☆☆☆
			☐	☐	☐	☆☆☆☆☆
			☐	☐	☐	☆☆☆☆☆
			☐	☐	☐	☆☆☆☆☆
			☐	☐	☐	☆☆☆☆☆
			☐	☐	☐	☆☆☆☆☆

BOOK LOG

KEEP TRACK OF YOUR BOOKS IN ONE PLACE!

#	TITLE	AUTHOR	SERIES?	RECOMMEND?	ABANDONNED?	RATING (1-5)
			☐	☐	☐	☆☆☆☆☆
			☐	☐	☐	☆☆☆☆☆
			☐	☐	☐	☆☆☆☆☆
			☐	☐	☐	☆☆☆☆☆
			☐	☐	☐	☆☆☆☆☆
			☐	☐	☐	☆☆☆☆☆
			☐	☐	☐	☆☆☆☆☆
			☐	☐	☐	☆☆☆☆☆
			☐	☐	☐	☆☆☆☆☆
			☐	☐	☐	☆☆☆☆☆
			☐	☐	☐	☆☆☆☆☆
			☐	☐	☐	☆☆☆☆☆
			☐	☐	☐	☆☆☆☆☆
			☐	☐	☐	☆☆☆☆☆
			☐	☐	☐	☆☆☆☆☆
			☐	☐	☐	☆☆☆☆☆
			☐	☐	☐	☆☆☆☆☆
			☐	☐	☐	☆☆☆☆☆
			☐	☐	☐	☆☆☆☆☆
			☐	☐	☐	☆☆☆☆☆
			☐	☐	☐	☆☆☆☆☆

BOOK LOG

KEEP TRACK OF YOUR BOOKS IN ONE PLACE!

#	TITLE	AUTHOR	SERIES?	RECOMMEND?	ABANDONNED?	RATING (1-5)
			☐	☐	☐	☆☆☆☆☆
			☐	☐	☐	☆☆☆☆☆
			☐	☐	☐	☆☆☆☆☆
			☐	☐	☐	☆☆☆☆☆
			☐	☐	☐	☆☆☆☆☆
			☐	☐	☐	☆☆☆☆☆
			☐	☐	☐	☆☆☆☆☆
			☐	☐	☐	☆☆☆☆☆
			☐	☐	☐	☆☆☆☆☆
			☐	☐	☐	☆☆☆☆☆
			☐	☐	☐	☆☆☆☆☆
			☐	☐	☐	☆☆☆☆☆
			☐	☐	☐	☆☆☆☆☆
			☐	☐	☐	☆☆☆☆☆
			☐	☐	☐	☆☆☆☆☆
			☐	☐	☐	☆☆☆☆☆
			☐	☐	☐	☆☆☆☆☆
			☐	☐	☐	☆☆☆☆☆
			☐	☐	☐	☆☆☆☆☆
			☐	☐	☐	☆☆☆☆☆
			☐	☐	☐	☆☆☆☆☆
			☐	☐	☐	☆☆☆☆☆

BOOK LOG
KEEP TRACK OF YOUR BOOKS IN ONE PLACE!

#	TITLE	AUTHOR	SERIES?	RECOMMEND?	ABANDONNED?	RATING (1-5)
			☐	☐	☐	☆☆☆☆☆
			☐	☐	☐	☆☆☆☆☆
			☐	☐	☐	☆☆☆☆☆
			☐	☐	☐	☆☆☆☆☆
			☐	☐	☐	☆☆☆☆☆
			☐	☐	☐	☆☆☆☆☆
			☐	☐	☐	☆☆☆☆☆
			☐	☐	☐	☆☆☆☆☆
			☐	☐	☐	☆☆☆☆☆
			☐	☐	☐	☆☆☆☆☆
			☐	☐	☐	☆☆☆☆☆
			☐	☐	☐	☆☆☆☆☆
			☐	☐	☐	☆☆☆☆☆
			☐	☐	☐	☆☆☆☆☆
			☐	☐	☐	☆☆☆☆☆
			☐	☐	☐	☆☆☆☆☆
			☐	☐	☐	☆☆☆☆☆
			☐	☐	☐	☆☆☆☆☆
			☐	☐	☐	☆☆☆☆☆
			☐	☐	☐	☆☆☆☆☆
			☐	☐	☐	☆☆☆☆☆
			☐	☐	☐	☆☆☆☆☆

BOOK LOG

KEEP TRACK OF YOUR BOOKS IN ONE PLACE!

#	TITLE	AUTHOR	SERIES?	RECOMMEND?	ABANDONNED?	RATING (1-5)
			☐	☐	☐	☆☆☆☆☆
			☐	☐	☐	☆☆☆☆☆
			☐	☐	☐	☆☆☆☆☆
			☐	☐	☐	☆☆☆☆☆
			☐	☐	☐	☆☆☆☆☆
			☐	☐	☐	☆☆☆☆☆
			☐	☐	☐	☆☆☆☆☆
			☐	☐	☐	☆☆☆☆☆
			☐	☐	☐	☆☆☆☆☆
			☐	☐	☐	☆☆☆☆☆
			☐	☐	☐	☆☆☆☆☆
			☐	☐	☐	☆☆☆☆☆
			☐	☐	☐	☆☆☆☆☆
			☐	☐	☐	☆☆☆☆☆
			☐	☐	☐	☆☆☆☆☆
			☐	☐	☐	☆☆☆☆☆
			☐	☐	☐	☆☆☆☆☆
			☐	☐	☐	☆☆☆☆☆
			☐	☐	☐	☆☆☆☆☆
			☐	☐	☐	☆☆☆☆☆
			☐	☐	☐	☆☆☆☆☆
			☐	☐	☐	☆☆☆☆☆

BOOK LOG

KEEP TRACK OF YOUR BOOKS IN ONE PLACE!

#	TITLE	AUTHOR	SERIES?	RECOMMEND?	ABANDONNED?	RATING (1-5)
			☐	☐	☐	☆☆☆☆☆
			☐	☐	☐	☆☆☆☆☆
			☐	☐	☐	☆☆☆☆☆
			☐	☐	☐	☆☆☆☆☆
			☐	☐	☐	☆☆☆☆☆
			☐	☐	☐	☆☆☆☆☆
			☐	☐	☐	☆☆☆☆☆
			☐	☐	☐	☆☆☆☆☆
			☐	☐	☐	☆☆☆☆☆
			☐	☐	☐	☆☆☆☆☆
			☐	☐	☐	☆☆☆☆☆
			☐	☐	☐	☆☆☆☆☆
			☐	☐	☐	☆☆☆☆☆
			☐	☐	☐	☆☆☆☆☆
			☐	☐	☐	☆☆☆☆☆
			☐	☐	☐	☆☆☆☆☆
			☐	☐	☐	☆☆☆☆☆
			☐	☐	☐	☆☆☆☆☆
			☐	☐	☐	☆☆☆☆☆
			☐	☐	☐	☆☆☆☆☆
			☐	☐	☐	☆☆☆☆☆

BOOK LOG

KEEP TRACK OF YOUR BOOKS IN ONE PLACE!

#	TITLE	AUTHOR	SERIES?	RECOMMEND?	ABANDONNED?	RATING (1-5)
			☐	☐	☐	☆☆☆☆☆
			☐	☐	☐	☆☆☆☆☆
			☐	☐	☐	☆☆☆☆☆
			☐	☐	☐	☆☆☆☆☆
			☐	☐	☐	☆☆☆☆☆
			☐	☐	☐	☆☆☆☆☆
			☐	☐	☐	☆☆☆☆☆
			☐	☐	☐	☆☆☆☆☆
			☐	☐	☐	☆☆☆☆☆
			☐	☐	☐	☆☆☆☆☆
			☐	☐	☐	☆☆☆☆☆
			☐	☐	☐	☆☆☆☆☆
			☐	☐	☐	☆☆☆☆☆
			☐	☐	☐	☆☆☆☆☆
			☐	☐	☐	☆☆☆☆☆
			☐	☐	☐	☆☆☆☆☆
			☐	☐	☐	☆☆☆☆☆
			☐	☐	☐	☆☆☆☆☆
			☐	☐	☐	☆☆☆☆☆
			☐	☐	☐	☆☆☆☆☆
			☐	☐	☐	☆☆☆☆☆
			☐	☐	☐	☆☆☆☆☆

BOOK LOG
KEEP TRACK OF YOUR BOOKS IN ONE PLACE!

#	TITLE	AUTHOR	SERIES?	RECOMMEND?	ABANDONNED?	RATING (1-5)
			☐	☐	☐	☆☆☆☆☆
			☐	☐	☐	☆☆☆☆☆
			☐	☐	☐	☆☆☆☆☆
			☐	☐	☐	☆☆☆☆☆
			☐	☐	☐	☆☆☆☆☆
			☐	☐	☐	☆☆☆☆☆
			☐	☐	☐	☆☆☆☆☆
			☐	☐	☐	☆☆☆☆☆
			☐	☐	☐	☆☆☆☆☆
			☐	☐	☐	☆☆☆☆☆
			☐	☐	☐	☆☆☆☆☆
			☐	☐	☐	☆☆☆☆☆
			☐	☐	☐	☆☆☆☆☆
			☐	☐	☐	☆☆☆☆☆
			☐	☐	☐	☆☆☆☆☆
			☐	☐	☐	☆☆☆☆☆
			☐	☐	☐	☆☆☆☆☆
			☐	☐	☐	☆☆☆☆☆
			☐	☐	☐	☆☆☆☆☆
			☐	☐	☐	☆☆☆☆☆
			☐	☐	☐	☆☆☆☆☆

FAVORITE BOOKS

FAVORITE BOOKS

FAVORITE BOOKS
EASILY FIND THOSE HIDDEN GEMS AGAIN!

#	TITLE	AUTHOR	NOTES

FAVORITE BOOKS
EASILY FIND THOSE HIDDEN GEMS AGAIN!

#	TITLE	AUTHOR	NOTES

FAVORITE BOOKS

EASILY FIND THOSE HIDDEN GEMS AGAIN!

#	TITLE	AUTHOR	NOTES

FAVORITE BOOKS
EASILY FIND THOSE HIDDEN GEMS AGAIN!

#	TITLE	AUTHOR	NOTES

FAVORITE BOOKS
EASILY FIND THOSE HIDDEN GEMS AGAIN!

#	TITLE	AUTHOR	NOTES

FAVORITE BOOKS
EASILY FIND THOSE HIDDEN GEMS AGAIN!

#	TITLE	AUTHOR	NOTES

FAVORITE QUOTES

FAVORITE QUOTES

FAVORITE QUOTES
NEVER LOSE THOSE SPECIAL MOMENTS

#	BOOK TITLE/SERIES TITLE	AUTHOR

QUOTE(S)

#	BOOK TITLE/SERIES TITLE	AUTHOR

QUOTE(S)

#	BOOK TITLE/SERIES TITLE	AUTHOR

QUOTE(S)

#	BOOK TITLE/SERIES TITLE	AUTHOR

QUOTE(S)

FAVORITE QUOTES

NEVER LOSE THOSE SPECIAL MOMENTS

#	BOOK TITLE/SERIES TITLE	AUTHOR

QUOTE(S)

#	BOOK TITLE/SERIES TITLE	AUTHOR

QUOTE(S)

#	BOOK TITLE/SERIES TITLE	AUTHOR

QUOTE(S)

#	BOOK TITLE/SERIES TITLE	AUTHOR

QUOTE(S)

FAVORITE QUOTES
NEVER LOSE THOSE SPECIAL MOMENTS

#	BOOK TITLE/SERIES TITLE	AUTHOR

QUOTE(S)

#	BOOK TITLE/SERIES TITLE	AUTHOR

QUOTE(S)

#	BOOK TITLE/SERIES TITLE	AUTHOR

QUOTE(S)

#	BOOK TITLE/SERIES TITLE	AUTHOR

QUOTE(S)

FAVORITE QUOTES
NEVER LOSE THOSE SPECIAL MOMENTS

#	BOOK TITLE/SERIES TITLE	AUTHOR

QUOTE(S)

#	BOOK TITLE/SERIES TITLE	AUTHOR

QUOTE(S)

#	BOOK TITLE/SERIES TITLE	AUTHOR

QUOTE(S)

#	BOOK TITLE/SERIES TITLE	AUTHOR

QUOTE(S)

FAVORITE QUOTES
NEVER LOSE THOSE SPECIAL MOMENTS

#	BOOK TITLE/SERIES TITLE	AUTHOR

QUOTE(S)

#	BOOK TITLE/SERIES TITLE	AUTHOR

QUOTE(S)

#	BOOK TITLE/SERIES TITLE	AUTHOR

QUOTE(S)

#	BOOK TITLE/SERIES TITLE	AUTHOR

QUOTE(S)

FAVORITE QUOTES
NEVER LOSE THOSE SPECIAL MOMENTS

#	BOOK TITLE/SERIES TITLE	AUTHOR

QUOTE(S)

#	BOOK TITLE/SERIES TITLE	AUTHOR

QUOTE(S)

#	BOOK TITLE/SERIES TITLE	AUTHOR

QUOTE(S)

#	BOOK TITLE/SERIES TITLE	AUTHOR

QUOTE(S)

READING TRACKER

READING TRACKER

READING TRACKER
COLOR THE STORY OF YOUR READING LIFE!

DAY	JAN	FEB	MAR	APR	MAY	JUN
1						
2						
3						
4						
5						
6						
7						
8						
9						
10						
11						
12						
13						
14						
15						
16						
17						
18						
19						
20						
21						
22						
23						
24						
25						
26						
27						
28						
29						
30						
31						

☐ 0-15 PAGES	☐ 45-60 PAGES	☐ 90-105 PAGES
☐ 15-30 PAGES	☐ 60-75 PAGES	☐ 105-120 PAGES
☐ 30-45 PAGES	☐ 75-90 PAGES	☐ 120+ PAGES

READING TRACKER
COLOR THE STORY OF YOUR READING LIFE!

DAY	JUL	AUG	SEPT	OCT	NOV	DEC
1						
2						
3						
4						
5						
6						
7						
8						
9						
10						
11						
12						
13						
14						
15						
16						
17						
18						
19						
20						
21						
22						
23						
24						
25						
26						
27						
28						
29						
30						
31						

- ☐ 0-15 PAGES
- ☐ 15-30 PAGES
- ☐ 30-45 PAGES
- ☐ 45-60 PAGES
- ☐ 60-75 PAGES
- ☐ 75-90 PAGES
- ☐ 90-105 PAGES
- ☐ 105-120 PAGES
- ☐ 120+ PAGES

CHALLENGES

CHALLENGES

BOOK BINGO

BINGO YOUR WAY THROUGH THE BOOKSHELF!

SET IN A FOREIGN LAND	TRUE CRIME	AWARD WINNER	A COLOR IN THE TITLE	UNDER 200 PAGES
YOUR FAVORITE GENRE	NEW-TO-YOU CULTURE	ANIMAL ON THE COVER	MADE INTO A SHOW	FOREIGN AUTHOR
ONE-WORD TITLE	NON-FICTION	PUBLISHED THIS YEAR	A SEQUEL	SET IN YOUR REGION
FANTASY BOOK	A FACE ON THE COVER	A CLASSIC	HISTORIC SETTING	NEW-TO-YOU GENRE
MADE INTO A MOVIE	OVER 500 PAGES	NEW-TO-YOU AUTHOR	YOUR CHOICE	NUMBER IN THE TITLE

ALPHABET CHALLENGE

YOUR READING QUEST STARTS NOW!

A
B
C
D
E
F
G
H
I
J
K
L
M
N
O
P
Q
R
S
T
U
V
W
X
Y
Z

100 BOOK CHALLENGE

100 BOOKS? CHALLENGE ACCEPTED!

100 BOOK CHALLENGE

TURN PAGES, WIN BRAGGING RIGHTS!

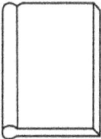

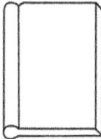

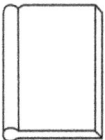

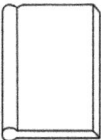

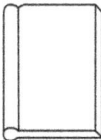

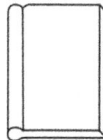

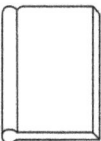

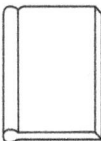

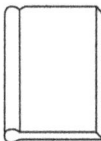

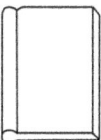

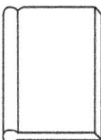

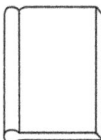

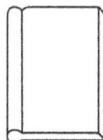

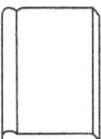

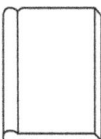

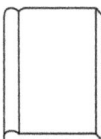

100 BOOK CHALLENGE
ONE BOOK CLOSER TO VICTORY!

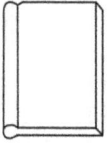

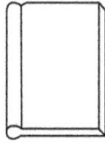

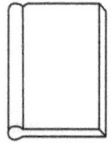

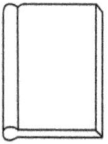

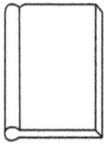

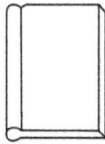

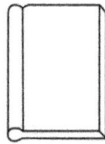

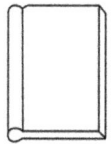

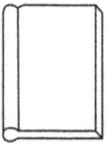

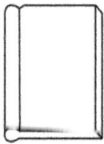

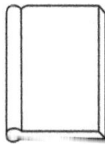

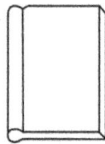

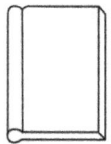

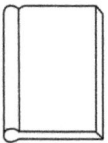

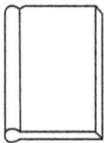

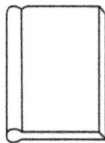

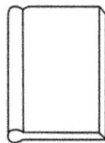

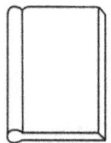

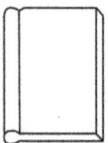

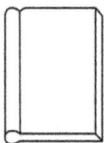

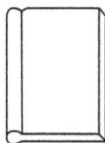

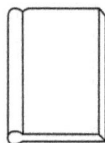

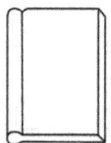

100 BOOK CHALLENGE
READ IT. CHECK IT. CONQUER THE CHALLENGE!

BOOK OF THE MONTH

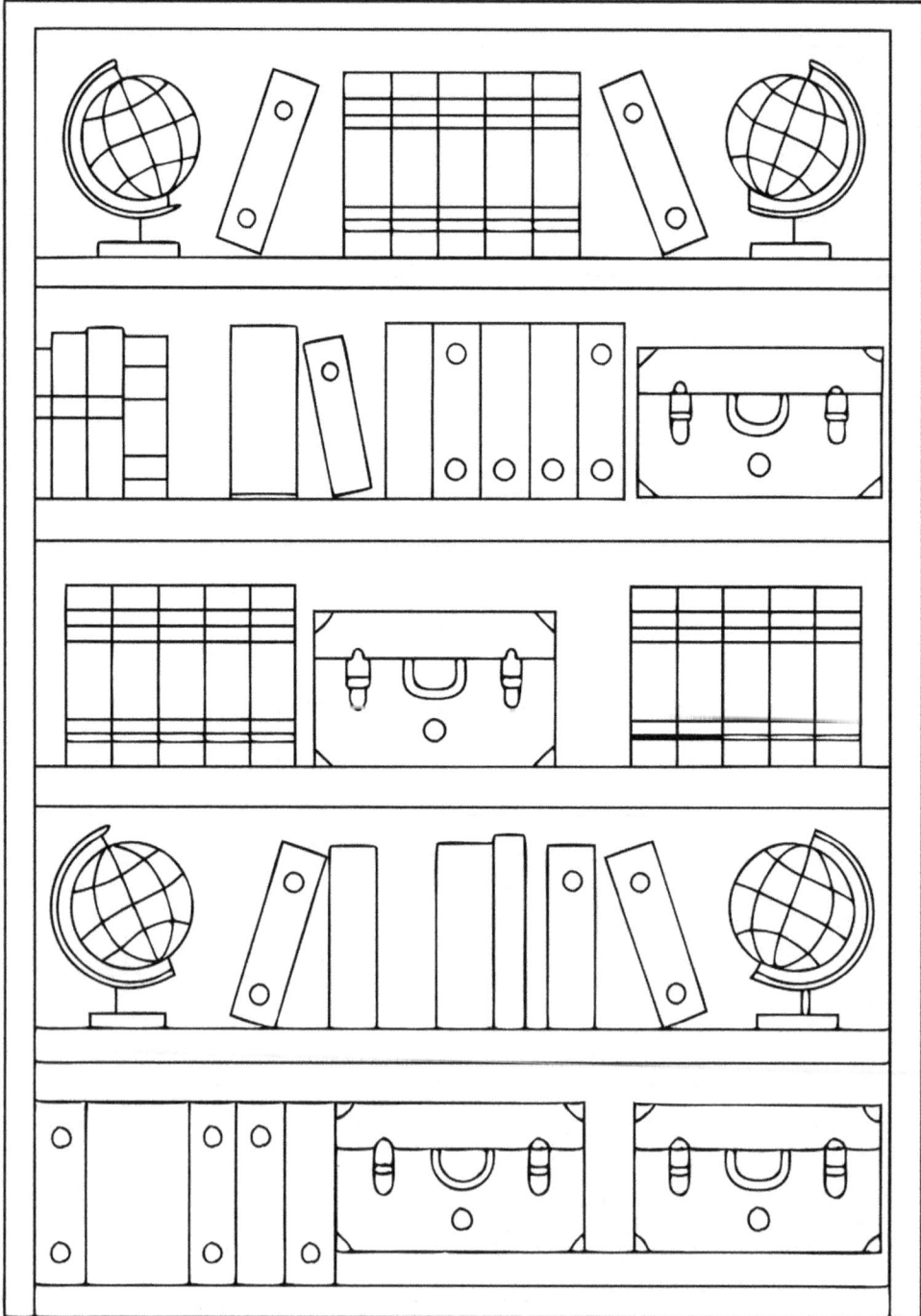

BOOK OF THE MONTH

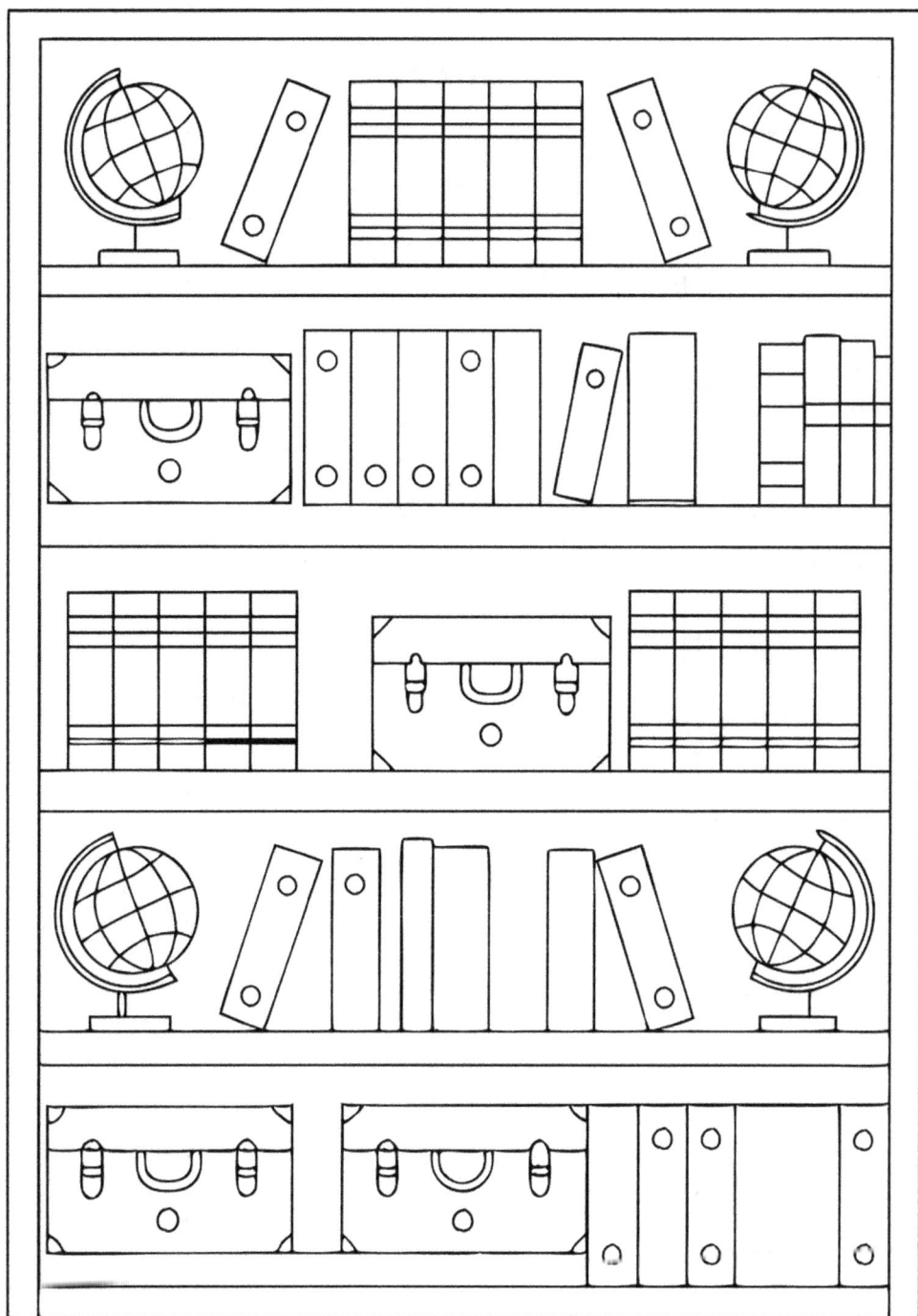

BOOK OF THE MONTH
A YEAR OF PAGES, A YEAR OF POSSIBILITIES.

JANUARY

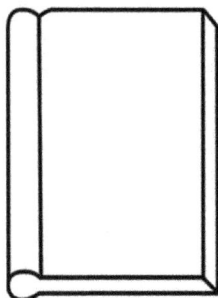

TITLE

AUTHOR

GENRE

QUOTE

FEBRUARY

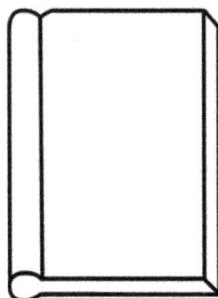

TITLE

AUTHOR

GENRE

QUOTE

MARCH

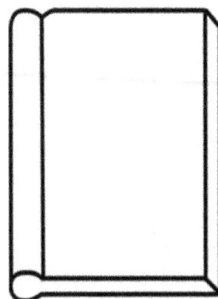

TITLE

AUTHOR

GENRE

QUOTE

BOOK OF THE MONTH
BOOKED EVERY MONTH, INSPIRED ALL YEAR.

APRIL

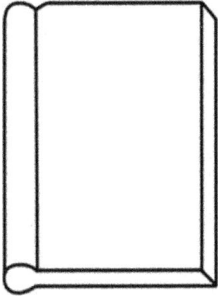

TITLE

AUTHOR

GENRE

QUOTE

MAY

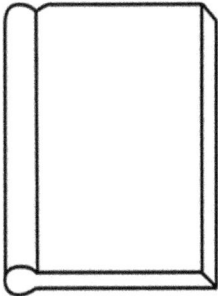

TITLE

AUTHOR

GENRE

QUOTE

JUNE

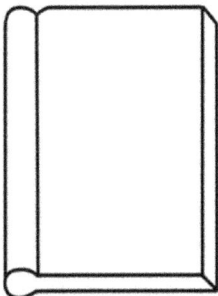

TITLE

AUTHOR

GENRE

QUOTE

BOOK OF THE MONTH

12 MONTHS. 12 BOOKS.
ONE INCREDIBLE READING JOURNEY.

JULY

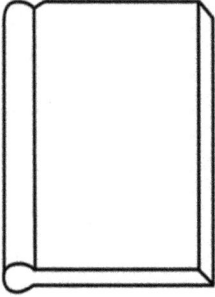

TITLE

AUTHOR

GENRE

QUOTE

AUGUST

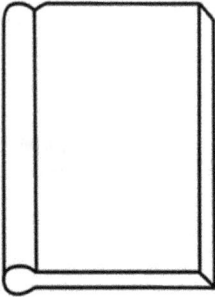

TITLE

AUTHOR

GENRE

QUOTE

SEPTEMBER

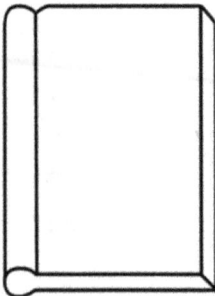

TITLE

AUTHOR

GENRE

QUOTE

BOOK OF THE MONTH

EVERY MONTH HAD A STORY—
TOGETHER THEY TOLD A YEAR.

OCTOBER

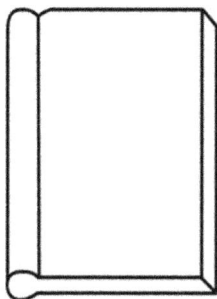

TITLE

AUTHOR

GENRE

QUOTE

NOVEMBER

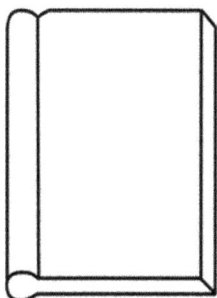

TITLE

AUTHOR

GENRE

QUOTE

DECEMBER

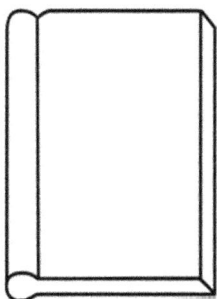

TITLE

AUTHOR

GENRE

QUOTE

BOOK OF THE YEAR

BOOK OF THE YEAR

BOOK OF THE YEAR
TWELVE MONTHS. TWELVE STORIES.
ONE EPIC YEAR OF READING.

JANUARY

FEBRUARY

MARCH

APRIL

MAY

JUNE

JULY

AUGUST

SEPTEMBER

OCTOBER

NOVEMBER

DECEMBER

BOOK OF THE YEAR
THE READ THAT LEFT A MARK—BOOK OF THE YEAR!

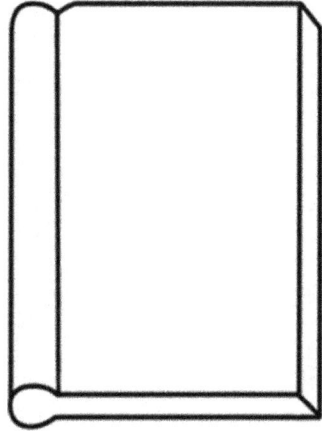

TITLE

AUTHOR

GENRE

QUOTE

BOOK REVIEWS

BOOK REVIEWS

BOOK REVIEW

#

TITLE	AUTHOR

☐ FICTION   GENRE   FIRST PUBLISHED
☐ NON-FICTION

NEW-TO-ME AUTHOR?   PAGE COUNT   FORMAT ☐ HARDCOVER ☐ PAPERBACK ☐ EBOOK ☐ AUDIOBOOK

☐ YES   ☐ NO   SOURCE ☐ BOUGHT ☐ BORROWED ☐ GIFTED ☐ OTHER _____

STARTED BOOK

_____

FINISHED BOOK

_____

WOULD RECOMMEND?
☐ YES   ☐ NO   ☐ MAYBE

RECOMMEND TO

_____

WOULD READ AGAIN?
☐ YES   ☐ NO   ☐ MAYBE

WOULD READ OTHER AUTHOR'S BOOKS?
☐ YES   ☐ NO   ☐ MAYBE

BOOK RATING

EASE OF READING
☆☆☆☆☆

CHARACTERS
☆☆☆☆☆

PLOT
☆☆☆☆☆

ENJOYABILITY
☆☆☆☆☆

OVERALL RATING
☆☆☆☆☆

DESCRIBE THE BOOK IN ONE SENTENCE
_____

WHAT DREW ME TO THIS BOOK?
_____

QUOTES/FAVORITE PASSAGES
_____
_____
_____
_____
_____
_____
_____

REVIEW
_____
_____
_____
_____
_____
_____
_____
_____
_____

BOOK REVIEW

#

TITLE	AUTHOR

☐ FICTION   GENRE   FIRST PUBLISHED
☐ NON-FICTION   _____   _____

NEW-TO-ME AUTHOR?   **PAGE COUNT**   **FORMAT** ☐ HARDCOVER ☐ PAPERBACK ☐ EBOOK ☐ AUDIOBOOK

☐   ☐   _____   **SOURCE** ☐ BOUGHT ☐ BORROWED ☐ GIFTED ☐ OTHER _____
YES   NO

DESCRIBE THE BOOK IN ONE SENTENCE

_____

WHAT DREW ME TO THIS BOOK?

_____

QUOTES/FAVORITE PASSAGES

_____
_____
_____
_____
_____
_____

REVIEW

_____
_____
_____
_____
_____
_____
_____
_____

STARTED BOOK

_____

FINISHED BOOK

_____

WOULD RECOMMEND?
☐ YES   ☐ NO   ☐ MAYBE
RECOMMEND TO

_____

WOULD READ AGAIN?
☐ YES   ☐ NO   ☐ MAYBE

WOULD READ OTHER AUTHOR'S BOOKS?
☐ YES   ☐ NO   ☐ MAYBE

BOOK RATING

EASE OF READING
☆☆☆☆☆

CHARACTERS
☆☆☆☆☆

PLOT
☆☆☆☆☆

ENJOYABILITY
☆☆☆☆☆

OVERALL RATING
☆☆☆☆☆

BOOK REVIEW

#

TITLE	AUTHOR

☐ FICTION   GENRE   FIRST PUBLISHED
☐ NON-FICTION _____   _____

NEW-TO-ME AUTHOR?   **PAGE COUNT**

☐   ☐
YES   NO   _____

FORMAT ☐ HARDCOVER ☐ PAPERBACK ☐ EBOOK ☐ AUDIOBOOK

SOURCE ☐ BOUGHT ☐ BORROWED ☐ GIFTED ☐ OTHER _____

STARTED BOOK

_____

FINISHED BOOK

_____

WOULD RECOMMEND?

☐ YES   ☐ NO   ☐ MAYBE

RECOMMEND TO

_____

WOULD READ AGAIN?

☐ YES   ☐ NO   ☐ MAYBE

WOULD READ OTHER AUTHOR'S BOOKS?

☐ YES   ☐ NO   ☐ MAYBE

BOOK RATING

EASE OF READING

☆☆☆☆☆

CHARACTERS

☆☆☆☆☆

PLOT

☆☆☆☆☆

ENJOYABILITY

☆☆☆☆☆

OVERALL RATING

☆☆☆☆☆

DESCRIBE THE BOOK IN ONE SENTENCE

_____

WHAT DREW ME TO THIS BOOK?

_____

QUOTES/FAVORITE PASSAGES

_____
_____
_____
_____
_____
_____
_____

REVIEW

_____
_____
_____
_____
_____
_____
_____
_____
_____

BOOK REVIEW

_____

TITLE	AUTHOR

☐ FICTION   GENRE   FIRST PUBLISHED
☐ NON-FICTION _____   _____

NEW-TO-ME AUTHOR?   **PAGE COUNT**   FORMAT ☐ HARDCOVER ☐ PAPERBACK ☐ EBOOK ☐ AUDIOBOOK

☐ ☐   _____   SOURCE ☐ BOUGHT ☐ BORROWED ☐ GIFTED ☐ OTHER _____
YES NO

DESCRIBE THE BOOK IN ONE SENTENCE

WHAT DREW ME TO THIS BOOK?

QUOTES/FAVORITE PASSAGES

REVIEW

STARTED BOOK

FINISHED BOOK

WOULD RECOMMEND?
☐ YES   ☐ NO   ☐ MAYBE
RECOMMEND TO

WOULD READ AGAIN?
☐ YES   ☐ NO   ☐ MAYBE

WOULD READ OTHER AUTHOR'S BOOKS?
☐ YES   ☐ NO   ☐ MAYBE

BOOK RATING

EASE OF READING
☆☆☆☆☆

CHARACTERS
☆☆☆☆☆

PLOT
☆☆☆☆☆

ENJOYABILITY
☆☆☆☆☆

OVERALL RATING
☆☆☆☆☆

BOOK REVIEW

#

TITLE	AUTHOR

☐ FICTION GENRE
☐ NON-FICTION _____ FIRST PUBLISHED

NEW-TO-ME
AUTHOR?
☐ YES ☐ NO

PAGE
COUNT
_____

FORMAT ☐ HARDCOVER ☐ PAPERBACK ☐ EBOOK ☐ AUDIOBOOK

SOURCE ☐ BOUGHT ☐ BORROWED ☐ GIFTED ☐ OTHER _____

STARTED BOOK

FINISHED BOOK

WOULD RECOMMEND?
☐ YES ☐ NO ☐ MAYBE
RECOMMEND TO

WOULD READ AGAIN?
☐ YES ☐ NO ☐ MAYBE

WOULD READ OTHER
AUTHOR'S BOOKS?
☐ YES ☐ NO ☐ MAYBE

BOOK RATING

EASE OF READING
☆☆☆☆☆

CHARACTERS
☆☆☆☆☆

PLOT
☆☆☆☆☆

ENJOYABILITY
☆☆☆☆☆

OVERALL RATING
☆☆☆☆☆

DESCRIBE THE BOOK IN ONE SENTENCE

WHAT DREW ME TO THIS BOOK?

QUOTES/FAVORITE PASSAGES

REVIEW

BOOK REVIEW

____

TITLE	AUTHOR

☐ FICTION   GENRE   FIRST PUBLISHED
☐ NON-FICTION   _____   _____

NEW-TO-ME AUTHOR?   PAGE COUNT   FORMAT ☐ HARDCOVER ☐ PAPERBACK ☐ EBOOK ☐ AUDIOBOOK

☐ YES ☐ NO   _____   SOURCE ☐ BOUGHT ☐ BORROWED ☐ GIFTED ☐ OTHER _____

DESCRIBE THE BOOK IN ONE SENTENCE
_____

WHAT DREW ME TO THIS BOOK?
_____

QUOTES/FAVORITE PASSAGES
_____
_____
_____
_____
_____
_____

REVIEW
_____
_____
_____
_____
_____
_____
_____
_____

STARTED BOOK
_____

FINISHED BOOK
_____

WOULD RECOMMEND?
☐ YES   ☐ NO   ☐ MAYBE

RECOMMEND TO
_____

WOULD READ AGAIN?
☐ YES   ☐ NO   ☐ MAYBE

WOULD READ OTHER AUTHOR'S BOOKS?
☐ YES   ☐ NO   ☐ MAYBE

BOOK RATING

EASE OF READING
☆☆☆☆☆

CHARACTERS
☆☆☆☆☆

PLOT
☆☆☆☆☆

ENJOYABILITY
☆☆☆☆☆

OVERALL RATING
☆☆☆☆☆

BOOK REVIEW

_____

TITLE	AUTHOR

☐ FICTION   GENRE   FIRST PUBLISHED
☐ NON-FICTION _____   _____

NEW-TO-ME AUTHOR?   PAGE COUNT   FORMAT ☐ HARDCOVER ☐ PAPERBACK ☐ EBOOK ☐ AUDIOBOOK

☐ YES ☐ NO   _____   SOURCE ☐ BOUGHT ☐ BORROWED ☐ GIFTED ☐ OTHER _____

STARTED BOOK
_____

FINISHED BOOK
_____

WOULD RECOMMEND?
☐ YES ☐ NO ☐ MAYBE
RECOMMEND TO
_____

WOULD READ AGAIN?
☐ YES ☐ NO ☐ MAYBE

WOULD READ OTHER AUTHOR'S BOOKS?
☐ YES ☐ NO ☐ MAYBE

BOOK RATING

EASE OF READING
☆☆☆☆☆

CHARACTERS
☆☆☆☆☆

PLOT
☆☆☆☆☆

ENJOYABILITY
☆☆☆☆☆

OVERALL RATING
☆☆☆☆☆

DESCRIBE THE BOOK IN ONE SENTENCE
_____

WHAT DREW ME TO THIS BOOK?
_____

QUOTES/FAVORITE PASSAGES
_____
_____
_____
_____
_____
_____

REVIEW
_____
_____
_____
_____
_____
_____
_____
_____

BOOK REVIEW

#

TITLE	AUTHOR

☐ FICTION   GENRE   FIRST PUBLISHED
☐ NON-FICTION _____   _____

NEW-TO-ME AUTHOR?   **PAGE COUNT**   FORMAT ☐ HARDCOVER ☐ PAPERBACK ☐ EBOOK ☐ AUDIOBOOK

☐   ☐   _____   SOURCE ☐ BOUGHT ☐ BORROWED ☐ GIFTED ☐ OTHER _____
YES   NO

DESCRIBE THE BOOK IN ONE SENTENCE
_____

WHAT DREW ME TO THIS BOOK?
_____

QUOTES/FAVORITE PASSAGES
_____
_____
_____
_____
_____
_____

REVIEW
_____
_____
_____
_____
_____
_____
_____
_____

STARTED BOOK
_____

FINISHED BOOK
_____

WOULD RECOMMEND?
☐ YES   ☐ NO   ☐ MAYBE

RECOMMEND TO
_____

WOULD READ AGAIN?
☐ YES   ☐ NO   ☐ MAYBE

WOULD READ OTHER AUTHOR'S BOOKS?
☐ YES   ☐ NO   ☐ MAYBE

BOOK RATING

EASE OF READING
☆☆☆☆☆

CHARACTERS
☆☆☆☆☆

PLOT
☆☆☆☆☆

ENJOYABILITY
☆☆☆☆☆

OVERALL RATING
☆☆☆☆☆

BOOK REVIEW

_____

TITLE	AUTHOR

☐ FICTION   GENRE   FIRST PUBLISHED
☐ NON-FICTION _____ _____

NEW-TO-ME AUTHOR?   **PAGE COUNT**

FORMAT ☐ HARDCOVER ☐ PAPERBACK ☐ EBOOK ☐ AUDIOBOOK

☐ ☐
YES NO   _____

SOURCE ☐ BOUGHT ☐ BORROWED ☐ GIFTED ☐ OTHER _____

STARTED BOOK
_____

FINISHED BOOK
_____

WOULD RECOMMEND?
☐ YES   ☐ NO   ☐ MAYBE

RECOMMEND TO
_____

WOULD READ AGAIN?
☐ YES   ☐ NO   ☐ MAYBE

WOULD READ OTHER AUTHOR'S BOOKS?
☐ YES   ☐ NO   ☐ MAYBE

BOOK RATING

EASE OF READING
☆☆☆☆☆

CHARACTERS
☆☆☆☆☆

PLOT
☆☆☆☆☆

ENJOYABILITY
☆☆☆☆☆

OVERALL RATING
☆☆☆☆☆

DESCRIBE THE BOOK IN ONE SENTENCE
_____

WHAT DREW ME TO THIS BOOK?
_____

QUOTES/FAVORITE PASSAGES
_____
_____
_____
_____
_____
_____
_____

REVIEW
_____
_____
_____
_____
_____
_____
_____
_____
_____
_____

BOOK REVIEW

\#

TITLE	AUTHOR

☐ FICTION   GENRE   FIRST PUBLISHED
☐ NON-FICTION   _____   _____

NEW-TO-ME   PAGE   FORMAT ☐ HARDCOVER ☐ PAPERBACK ☐ EBOOK ☐ AUDIOBOOK
AUTHOR?   COUNT

☐   ☐   _____   SOURCE ☐ BOUGHT ☐ BORROWED ☐ GIFTED ☐ OTHER _____
YES   NO

DESCRIBE THE BOOK IN ONE SENTENCE

WHAT DREW ME TO THIS BOOK?

QUOTES/FAVORITE PASSAGES

REVIEW

STARTED BOOK

FINISHED BOOK

WOULD RECOMMEND?
☐ YES   ☐ NO   ☐ MAYBE

RECOMMEND TO

WOULD READ AGAIN?
☐ YES   ☐ NO   ☐ MAYBE

WOULD READ OTHER
AUTHOR'S BOOKS?
☐ YES   ☐ NO   ☐ MAYBE

BOOK RATING

EASE OF READING
☆☆☆☆☆

CHARACTERS
☆☆☆☆☆

PLOT
☆☆☆☆☆

ENJOYABILITY
☆☆☆☆☆

OVERALL RATING
☆☆☆☆☆

BOOK REVIEW

#

TITLE	AUTHOR

☐ FICTION GENRE FIRST PUBLISHED
☐ NON-FICTION _____ _____

NEW-TO-ME AUTHOR? PAGE COUNT

☐ ☐
YES NO _____

FORMAT ☐ HARDCOVER ☐ PAPERBACK ☐ EBOOK ☐ AUDIOBOOK

SOURCE ☐ BOUGHT ☐ BORROWED ☐ GIFTED ☐ OTHER _____

STARTED BOOK

_____

FINISHED BOOK

_____

WOULD RECOMMEND?
☐ YES ☐ NO ☐ MAYBE

RECOMMEND TO

_____

WOULD READ AGAIN?
☐ YES ☐ NO ☐ MAYBE

WOULD READ OTHER AUTHOR'S BOOKS?
☐ YES ☐ NO ☐ MAYBE

BOOK RATING

EASE OF READING
☆☆☆☆☆

CHARACTERS
☆☆☆☆☆

PLOT
☆☆☆☆☆

ENJOYABILITY
☆☆☆☆☆

OVERALL RATING
☆☆☆☆☆

DESCRIBE THE BOOK IN ONE SENTENCE

_____

WHAT DREW ME TO THIS BOOK?

_____

QUOTES/FAVORITE PASSAGES

_____
_____
_____
_____
_____
_____

REVIEW

_____
_____
_____
_____
_____
_____
_____
_____
_____

BOOK REVIEW

TITLE	AUTHOR

☐ FICTION   GENRE   FIRST PUBLISHED
☐ NON-FICTION _____   _____

NEW-TO-ME AUTHOR?   **PAGE COUNT**   FORMAT ☐ HARDCOVER ☐ PAPERBACK ☐ EBOOK ☐ AUDIOBOOK

☐ YES ☐ NO   _____   SOURCE ☐ BOUGHT ☐ BORROWED ☐ GIFTED ☐ OTHER _____

DESCRIBE THE BOOK IN ONE SENTENCE
_____

WHAT DREW ME TO THIS BOOK?
_____

QUOTES/FAVORITE PASSAGES
_____
_____
_____
_____
_____
_____

REVIEW
_____
_____
_____
_____
_____
_____
_____
_____

STARTED BOOK
_____

FINISHED BOOK
_____

WOULD RECOMMEND?
☐ YES   ☐ NO   ☐ MAYBE

RECOMMEND TO
_____

WOULD READ AGAIN?
☐ YES   ☐ NO   ☐ MAYBE

WOULD READ OTHER AUTHOR'S BOOKS?
☐ YES   ☐ NO   ☐ MAYBE

BOOK RATING

EASE OF READING
☆☆☆☆☆

CHARACTERS
☆☆☆☆☆

PLOT
☆☆☆☆☆

ENJOYABILITY
☆☆☆☆☆

OVERALL RATING
☆☆☆☆☆

BOOK REVIEW

TITLE	AUTHOR
#	

☐ FICTION
☐ NON-FICTION

GENERE _____

FIRST PUBLISHED _____

NEW-TO-ME AUTHOR?
☐ YES ☐ NO

PAGE COUNT
_____

FORMAT ☐ HARDCOVER ☐ PAPERBACK ☐ EBOOK ☐ AUDIOBOOK

SOURCE ☐ BOUGHT ☐ BORROWED ☐ GIFTED ☐ OTHER _____

STARTED BOOK
_____

FINISHED BOOK
_____

WOULD RECOMMEND?
☐ YES ☐ NO ☐ MAYBE

RECOMMEND TO
_____

WOULD READ AGAIN?
☐ YES ☐ NO ☐ MAYBE

WOULD READ OTHER AUTHOR'S BOOKS?
☐ YES ☐ NO ☐ MAYBE

BOOK RATING

EASE OF READING
☆☆☆☆☆

CHARACTERS
☆☆☆☆☆

PLOT
☆☆☆☆☆

ENJOYABILITY
☆☆☆☆☆

OVERALL RATING
☆☆☆☆☆

DESCRIBE THE BOOK IN ONE SENTENCE
_____

WHAT DREW ME TO THIS BOOK?
_____

QUOTES/FAVORITE PASSAGES
_____
_____
_____
_____
_____
_____
_____

REVIEW
_____
_____
_____
_____
_____
_____
_____
_____
_____

BOOK REVIEW

TITLE	AUTHOR

☐ FICTION　　　GENRE　　　　　　　　FIRST PUBLISHED
☐ NON-FICTION　_____　_____

NEW-TO-ME AUTHOR?　　PAGE COUNT　　FORMAT ☐ HARDCOVER ☐ PAPERBACK ☐ EBOOK ☐ AUDIOBOOK

☐ YES　☐ NO　　_____　SOURCE ☐ BOUGHT ☐ BORROWED ☐ GIFTED ☐ OTHER _____

DESCRIBE THE BOOK IN ONE SENTENCE
_____

WHAT DREW ME TO THIS BOOK?
_____

QUOTES/FAVORITE PASSAGES
_____
_____
_____
_____
_____
_____

REVIEW
_____
_____
_____
_____
_____
_____
_____
_____

STARTED BOOK
_____

FINISHED BOOK
_____

WOULD RECOMMEND?
☐ YES　☐ NO　☐ MAYBE
RECOMMEND TO
_____

WOULD READ AGAIN?
☐ YES　☐ NO　☐ MAYBE

WOULD READ OTHER AUTHOR'S BOOKS?
☐ YES　☐ NO　☐ MAYBE

BOOK RATING

EASE OF READING
☆☆☆☆☆

CHARACTERS
☆☆☆☆☆

PLOT
☆☆☆☆☆

ENJOYABILITY
☆☆☆☆☆

OVERALL RATING
☆☆☆☆☆

BOOK REVIEW

#

TITLE	AUTHOR

☐ FICTION   GENRE   FIRST PUBLISHED
☐ NON-FICTION   _____   _____

NEW-TO-ME   PAGE   FORMAT ☐ HARDCOVER ☐ PAPERBACK ☐ EBOOK ☐ AUDIOBOOK
AUTHOR?   COUNT
☐   ☐   SOURCE ☐ BOUGHT ☐ BORROWED ☐ GIFTED ☐ OTHER _____
YES   NO   _____

STARTED BOOK
_____

FINISHED BOOK
_____

WOULD RECOMMEND?
☐ YES   ☐ NO   ☐ MAYBE

RECOMMEND TO
_____

WOULD READ AGAIN?
☐ YES   ☐ NO   ☐ MAYBE

WOULD READ OTHER
AUTHOR'S BOOKS?
☐ YES   ☐ NO   ☐ MAYBE

BOOK RATING

EASE OF READING
☆☆☆☆☆

CHARACTERS
☆☆☆☆☆

PLOT
☆☆☆☆☆

ENJOYABILITY
☆☆☆☆☆

OVERALL RATING
☆☆☆☆☆

DESCRIBE THE BOOK IN ONE SENTENCE
_____

WHAT DREW ME TO THIS BOOK?
_____

QUOTES/FAVORITE PASSAGES
_____
_____
_____
_____
_____
_____

REVIEW
_____
_____
_____
_____
_____
_____
_____
_____
_____

BOOK REVIEW

TITLE	AUTHOR

☐ FICTION GENRE FIRST PUBLISHED
☐ NON-FICTION _____ _____

NEW-TO-ME AUTHOR?   PAGE COUNT   FORMAT ☐ HARDCOVER ☐ PAPERBACK ☐ EBOOK ☐ AUDIOBOOK

☐ YES ☐ NO   _____   SOURCE ☐ BOUGHT ☐ BORROWED ☐ GIFTED ☐ OTHER _____

DESCRIBE THE BOOK IN ONE SENTENCE

_____

WHAT DREW ME TO THIS BOOK?

_____

QUOTES/FAVORITE PASSAGES

_____
_____
_____
_____
_____
_____

REVIEW

_____
_____
_____
_____
_____
_____
_____
_____

STARTED BOOK

_____

FINISHED BOOK

_____

WOULD RECOMMEND?
☐ YES ☐ NO ☐ MAYBE

RECOMMEND TO

_____

WOULD READ AGAIN?
☐ YES ☐ NO ☐ MAYBE

WOULD READ OTHER AUTHOR'S BOOKS?
☐ YES ☐ NO ☐ MAYBE

BOOK RATING

EASE OF READING
☆☆☆☆☆

CHARACTERS
☆☆☆☆☆

PLOT
☆☆☆☆☆

ENJOYABILITY
☆☆☆☆☆

OVERALL RATING
☆☆☆☆☆

BOOK REVIEW

TITLE	AUTHOR

☐ FICTION   GENRE   FIRST PUBLISHED
☐ NON-FICTION   _____   _____

NEW-TO-ME AUTHOR?   **PAGE COUNT**   **FORMAT** ☐ HARDCOVER ☐ PAPERBACK ☐ EBOOK ☐ AUDIOBOOK

☐ YES   ☐ NO   _____   **SOURCE** ☐ BOUGHT ☐ BORROWED ☐ GIFTED ☐ OTHER _____

STARTED BOOK

_____

FINISHED BOOK

_____

WOULD RECOMMEND?
☐ YES   ☐ NO   ☐ MAYBE

RECOMMEND TO

_____

WOULD READ AGAIN?
☐ YES   ☐ NO   ☐ MAYBE

WOULD READ OTHER AUTHOR'S BOOKS?

☐ YES   ☐ NO   ☐ MAYBE

BOOK RATING

EASE OF READING
☆☆☆☆☆

CHARACTERS
☆☆☆☆☆

PLOT
☆☆☆☆☆

ENJOYABILITY
☆☆☆☆☆

OVERALL RATING
☆☆☆☆☆

DESCRIBE THE BOOK IN ONE SENTENCE

_____

WHAT DREW ME TO THIS BOOK?

_____

QUOTES/FAVORITE PASSAGES

_____

_____

_____

_____

_____

_____

REVIEW

_____

_____

_____

_____

_____

_____

_____

_____

_____

BOOK REVIEW

#

TITLE	AUTHOR

☐ FICTION   GENRE   FIRST PUBLISHED
☐ NON-FICTION   _____   _____

NEW-TO-ME   PAGE   FORMAT ☐ HARDCOVER ☐ PAPERBACK ☐ EBOOK ☐ AUDIOBOOK
AUTHOR?   COUNT

☐   ☐   _____   SOURCE ☐ BOUGHT ☐ BORROWED ☐ GIFTED ☐ OTHER _____
YES   NO

DESCRIBE THE BOOK IN ONE SENTENCE

_____

WHAT DREW ME TO THIS BOOK?

_____

QUOTES/FAVORITE PASSAGES

_____
_____
_____
_____
_____
_____

REVIEW

_____
_____
_____
_____
_____
_____
_____
_____

STARTED BOOK
_____

FINISHED BOOK
_____

WOULD RECOMMEND?
☐ YES   ☐ NO   ☐ MAYBE

RECOMMEND TO
_____

WOULD READ AGAIN?
☐ YES   ☐ NO   ☐ MAYBE

WOULD READ OTHER
AUTHOR'S BOOKS?
☐ YES   ☐ NO   ☐ MAYBE

BOOK RATING

EASE OF READING
☆☆☆☆☆

CHARACTERS
☆☆☆☆☆

PLOT
☆☆☆☆☆

ENJOYABILITY
☆☆☆☆☆

OVERALL RATING
☆☆☆☆☆

BOOK REVIEW

#

TITLE	AUTHOR

☐ FICTION
☐ NON-FICTION

GENRE

FIRST PUBLISHED

NEW-TO-ME AUTHOR?

☐ YES ☐ NO

PAGE COUNT

FORMAT ☐ HARDCOVER ☐ PAPERBACK ☐ EBOOK ☐ AUDIOBOOK

SOURCE ☐ BOUGHT ☐ BORROWED ☐ GIFTED ☐ OTHER _____

STARTED BOOK

FINISHED BOOK

WOULD RECOMMEND?
☐ YES ☐ NO ☐ MAYBE

RECOMMEND TO

WOULD READ AGAIN?
☐ YES ☐ NO ☐ MAYBE

WOULD READ OTHER AUTHOR'S BOOKS?
☐ YES ☐ NO ☐ MAYBE

BOOK RATING

EASE OF READING
☆☆☆☆☆

CHARACTERS
☆☆☆☆☆

PLOT
☆☆☆☆☆

ENJOYABILITY
☆☆☆☆☆

OVERALL RATING
☆☆☆☆☆

DESCRIBE THE BOOK IN ONE SENTENCE

WHAT DREW ME TO THIS BOOK?

QUOTES/FAVORITE PASSAGES

REVIEW

BOOK REVIEW

TITLE	AUTHOR

☐ FICTION   GENRE   FIRST PUBLISHED
☐ NON-FICTION   _____   _____

NEW-TO-ME AUTHOR?   **PAGE COUNT**   **FORMAT** ☐ HARDCOVER ☐ PAPERBACK ☐ EBOOK ☐ AUDIOBOOK

☐ YES   ☐ NO   _____   **SOURCE** ☐ BOUGHT ☐ BORROWED ☐ GIFTED ☐ OTHER _____

DESCRIBE THE BOOK IN ONE SENTENCE

_____

WHAT DREW ME TO THIS BOOK?

_____

QUOTES/FAVORITE PASSAGES

_____
_____
_____
_____
_____

REVIEW

_____
_____
_____
_____
_____
_____
_____
_____

STARTED BOOK

_____

FINISHED BOOK

_____

WOULD RECOMMEND?

☐ YES   ☐ NO   ☐ MAYBE

RECOMMEND TO

_____

WOULD READ AGAIN?

☐ YES   ☐ NO   ☐ MAYBE

WOULD READ OTHER AUTHOR'S BOOKS?

☐ YES   ☐ NO   ☐ MAYBE

BOOK RATING

EASE OF READING
☆☆☆☆☆

CHARACTERS
☆☆☆☆☆

PLOT
☆☆☆☆☆

ENJOYABILITY
☆☆☆☆☆

OVERALL RATING
☆☆☆☆☆

BOOK REVIEW

TITLE	AUTHOR

#

☐ FICTION   GENRE   FIRST PUBLISHED
☐ NON-FICTION _____   _____

NEW-TO-ME AUTHOR?   PAGE COUNT   FORMAT ☐ HARDCOVER ☐ PAPERBACK ☐ EBOOK ☐ AUDIOBOOK

☐ ☐   _____   SOURCE ☐ BOUGHT ☐ BORROWED ☐ GIFTED ☐ OTHER _____
YES NO

STARTED BOOK
_____

FINISHED BOOK
_____

WOULD RECOMMEND?
☐ YES   ☐ NO   ☐ MAYBE

RECOMMEND TO
_____

WOULD READ AGAIN?
☐ YES   ☐ NO   ☐ MAYBE

WOULD READ OTHER AUTHOR'S BOOKS?
☐ YES   ☐ NO   ☐ MAYBE

BOOK RATING

EASE OF READING
☆☆☆☆☆

CHARACTERS
☆☆☆☆☆

PLOT
☆☆☆☆☆

ENJOYABILITY
☆☆☆☆☆

OVERALL RATING
☆☆☆☆☆

DESCRIBE THE BOOK IN ONE SENTENCE
_____

WHAT DREW ME TO THIS BOOK?
_____

QUOTES/FAVORITE PASSAGES
_____
_____
_____
_____
_____
_____

REVIEW
_____
_____
_____
_____
_____
_____
_____
_____

BOOK REVIEW

#

TITLE	AUTHOR

☐ FICTION   GENRE   FIRST PUBLISHED
☐ NON-FICTION _____ _____

NEW-TO-ME AUTHOR?   PAGE COUNT   FORMAT ☐ HARDCOVER ☐ PAPERBACK ☐ EBOOK ☐ AUDIOBOOK

☐   ☐   _____   SOURCE ☐ BOUGHT ☐ BORROWED ☐ GIFTED ☐ OTHER _____
YES   NO

DESCRIBE THE BOOK IN ONE SENTENCE
_____

WHAT DREW ME TO THIS BOOK?
_____

QUOTES/FAVORITE PASSAGES
_____
_____
_____
_____
_____
_____

REVIEW
_____
_____
_____
_____
_____
_____
_____
_____

STARTED BOOK
_____

FINISHED BOOK
_____

WOULD RECOMMEND?
☐ YES   ☐ NO   ☐ MAYBE

RECOMMEND TO
_____

WOULD READ AGAIN?
☐ YES   ☐ NO   ☐ MAYBE

WOULD READ OTHER AUTHOR'S BOOKS?
☐ YES   ☐ NO   ☐ MAYBE

BOOK RATING

EASE OF READING
☆☆☆☆☆

CHARACTERS
☆☆☆☆☆

PLOT
☆☆☆☆☆

ENJOYABILITY
☆☆☆☆☆

OVERALL RATING
☆☆☆☆☆

BOOK REVIEW

#

TITLE	AUTHOR

☐ FICTION   GENRE   FIRST PUBLISHED
☐ NON-FICTION

NEW-TO-ME AUTHOR?   PAGE COUNT   FORMAT ☐ HARDCOVER ☐ PAPERBACK ☐ EBOOK ☐ AUDIOBOOK

☐ YES   ☐ NO   _____   SOURCE ☐ BOUGHT ☐ BORROWED ☐ GIFTED ☐ OTHER _____

STARTED BOOK

_____

FINISHED BOOK

_____

WOULD RECOMMEND?

☐ YES   ☐ NO   ☐ MAYBE

RECOMMEND TO

_____

WOULD READ AGAIN?

☐ YES   ☐ NO   ☐ MAYBE

WOULD READ OTHER AUTHOR'S BOOKS?

☐ YES   ☐ NO   ☐ MAYBE

BOOK RATING

EASE OF READING
☆☆☆☆☆

CHARACTERS
☆☆☆☆☆

PLOT
☆☆☆☆☆

ENJOYABILITY
☆☆☆☆☆

OVERALL RATING
☆☆☆☆☆

DESCRIBE THE BOOK IN ONE SENTENCE
_____

WHAT DREW ME TO THIS BOOK?
_____

QUOTES/FAVORITE PASSAGES
_____
_____
_____
_____
_____
_____

REVIEW
_____
_____
_____
_____
_____
_____
_____
_____
_____

BOOK REVIEW

TITLE	AUTHOR

☐ FICTION   GENRE   FIRST PUBLISHED
☐ NON-FICTION   _____   _____

NEW-TO-ME   PAGE   FORMAT ☐ HARDCOVER ☐ PAPERBACK ☐ EBOOK ☐ AUDIOBOOK
AUTHOR?   COUNT
☐   ☐   _____   SOURCE ☐ BOUGHT ☐ BORROWED ☐ GIFTED ☐ OTHER _____
YES   NO

DESCRIBE THE BOOK IN ONE SENTENCE
_____

WHAT DREW ME TO THIS BOOK?
_____

QUOTES/FAVORITE PASSAGES
_____
_____
_____
_____
_____
_____

REVIEW
_____
_____
_____
_____
_____
_____
_____
_____

STARTED BOOK
_____

FINISHED BOOK
_____

WOULD RECOMMEND?
☐ YES   ☐ NO   ☐ MAYBE
RECOMMEND TO
_____

WOULD READ AGAIN?
☐ YES   ☐ NO   ☐ MAYBE

WOULD READ OTHER
AUTHOR'S BOOKS?
☐ YES   ☐ NO   ☐ MAYBE

BOOK RATING

EASE OF READING
☆☆☆☆☆

CHARACTERS
☆☆☆☆☆

PLOT
☆☆☆☆☆

ENJOYABILITY
☆☆☆☆☆

OVERALL RATING
☆☆☆☆☆

BOOK REVIEW

#

TITLE		AUTHOR	

☐ FICTION   GENRE   FIRST PUBLISHED
☐ NON-FICTION _____ _____

NEW-TO-ME AUTHOR?   **PAGE COUNT**   FORMAT ☐ HARDCOVER ☐ PAPERBACK ☐ EBOOK ☐ AUDIOBOOK

☐   ☐   _____   SOURCE ☐ BOUGHT ☐ BORROWED ☐ GIFTED ☐ OTHER _____
YES   NO

STARTED BOOK

_____

FINISHED BOOK

_____

WOULD RECOMMEND?
☐ YES   ☐ NO   ☐ MAYBE

RECOMMEND TO

_____

WOULD READ AGAIN?
☐ YES   ☐ NO   ☐ MAYBE

WOULD READ OTHER AUTHOR'S BOOKS?

☐ YES   ☐ NO   ☐ MAYBE

BOOK RATING

EASE OF READING
☆☆☆☆☆

CHARACTERS
☆☆☆☆☆

PLOT
☆☆☆☆☆

ENJOYABILITY
☆☆☆☆☆

OVERALL RATING
☆☆☆☆☆

DESCRIBE THE BOOK IN ONE SENTENCE
_____

WHAT DREW ME TO THIS BOOK?
_____

QUOTES/FAVORITE PASSAGES
_____
_____
_____
_____
_____
_____
_____

REVIEW
_____
_____
_____
_____
_____
_____
_____
_____
_____

BOOK REVIEW

TITLE	AUTHOR

☐ FICTION   GENRE   FIRST PUBLISHED
☐ NON-FICTION   _____   _____

NEW-TO-ME AUTHOR?   **PAGE COUNT**   **FORMAT** ☐ HARDCOVER ☐ PAPERBACK ☐ EBOOK ☐ AUDIOBOOK

☐ YES   ☐ NO   _____   **SOURCE** ☐ BOUGHT ☐ BORROWED ☐ GIFTED ☐ OTHER _____

DESCRIBE THE BOOK IN ONE SENTENCE

WHAT DREW ME TO THIS BOOK?

QUOTES/FAVORITE PASSAGES

REVIEW

STARTED BOOK

FINISHED BOOK

WOULD RECOMMEND?
☐ YES   ☐ NO   ☐ MAYBE

RECOMMEND TO

WOULD READ AGAIN?
☐ YES   ☐ NO   ☐ MAYBE

WOULD READ OTHER AUTHOR'S BOOKS?
☐ YES   ☐ NO   ☐ MAYBE

BOOK RATING

EASE OF READING
☆☆☆☆☆

CHARACTERS
☆☆☆☆☆

PLOT
☆☆☆☆☆

ENJOYABILITY
☆☆☆☆☆

OVERALL RATING
☆☆☆☆☆

BOOK REVIEW

#

TITLE	AUTHOR

☐ FICTION   GENRE   FIRST PUBLISHED
☐ NON-FICTION _____ _____

NEW-TO-ME AUTHOR?   **PAGE COUNT**   FORMAT ☐ HARDCOVER ☐ PAPERBACK ☐ EBOOK ☐ AUDIOBOOK

☐ ☐   _____   SOURCE ☐ BOUGHT ☐ BORROWED ☐ GIFTED ☐ OTHER _____
YES NO

STARTED BOOK

_____

FINISHED BOOK

_____

WOULD RECOMMEND?
☐ YES   ☐ NO   ☐ MAYBE

RECOMMEND TO

_____

WOULD READ AGAIN?
☐ YES   ☐ NO   ☐ MAYBE

WOULD READ OTHER AUTHOR'S BOOKS?

☐ YES   ☐ NO   ☐ MAYBE

BOOK RATING

EASE OF READING
☆☆☆☆☆

CHARACTERS
☆☆☆☆☆

PLOT
☆☆☆☆☆

ENJOYABILITY
☆☆☆☆☆

OVERALL RATING
☆☆☆☆☆

DESCRIBE THE BOOK IN ONE SENTENCE

_____

WHAT DREW ME TO THIS BOOK?

_____

QUOTES/FAVORITE PASSAGES

_____
_____
_____
_____
_____
_____
_____

REVIEW

_____
_____
_____
_____
_____
_____
_____
_____
_____

BOOK REVIEW

#

TITLE	AUTHOR

☐ FICTION GENRE FIRST PUBLISHED
☐ NON-FICTION _____ _____

NEW-TO-ME AUTHOR? PAGE COUNT FORMAT ☐ HARDCOVER ☐ PAPERBACK ☐ EBOOK ☐ AUDIOBOOK
☐ YES ☐ NO _____ SOURCE ☐ BOUGHT ☐ BORROWED ☐ GIFTED ☐ OTHER _____

DESCRIBE THE BOOK IN ONE SENTENCE
_____

WHAT DREW ME TO THIS BOOK?
_____

QUOTES/FAVORITE PASSAGES
_____
_____
_____
_____
_____
_____

REVIEW
_____
_____
_____
_____
_____
_____
_____

STARTED BOOK
_____

FINISHED BOOK
_____

WOULD RECOMMEND?
☐ YES   ☐ NO   ☐ MAYBE

RECOMMEND TO
_____

WOULD READ AGAIN?
☐ YES   ☐ NO   ☐ MAYBE

WOULD READ OTHER AUTHOR'S BOOKS?
☐ YES   ☐ NO   ☐ MAYBE

BOOK RATING

EASE OF READING
☆☆☆☆☆

CHARACTERS
☆☆☆☆☆

PLOT
☆☆☆☆☆

ENJOYABILITY
☆☆☆☆☆

OVERALL RATING
☆☆☆☆☆

BOOK REVIEW

TITLE	AUTHOR

☐ FICTION   GENERE   FIRST PUBLISHED
☐ NON-FICTION _____ _____

NEW-TO-ME
AUTHOR?
☐ YES   ☐ NO

PAGE
COUNT
_____

FORMAT ☐ HARDCOVER ☐ PAPERBACK ☐ EBOOK ☐ AUDIOBOOK

SOURCE ☐ BOUGHT ☐ BORROWED ☐ GIFTED ☐ OTHER _____

STARTED BOOK

_____

FINISHED BOOK

_____

WOULD RECOMMEND?
☐ YES   ☐ NO   ☐ MAYBE

RECOMMEND TO

_____

WOULD READ AGAIN?
☐ YES   ☐ NO   ☐ MAYBE

WOULD READ OTHER
AUTHOR'S BOOKS?
☐ YES   ☐ NO   ☐ MAYBE

BOOK RATING

EASE OF READING
☆☆☆☆☆

CHARACTERS
☆☆☆☆☆

PLOT
☆☆☆☆☆

ENJOYABILITY
☆☆☆☆☆

OVERALL RATING
☆☆☆☆☆

DESCRIBE THE BOOK IN ONE SENTENCE

_____

WHAT DREW ME TO THIS BOOK?

_____

QUOTES/FAVORITE PASSAGES

_____
_____
_____
_____
_____

REVIEW

_____
_____
_____
_____
_____
_____
_____
_____

BOOK REVIEW

TITLE	AUTHOR

☐ FICTION   GENRE   FIRST PUBLISHED
☐ NON-FICTION _____ _____

NEW-TO-ME AUTHOR?   **PAGE COUNT**   **FORMAT** ☐ HARDCOVER ☐ PAPERBACK ☐ EBOOK ☐ AUDIOBOOK

☐ YES   ☐ NO   _____   **SOURCE** ☐ BOUGHT ☐ BORROWED ☐ GIFTED ☐ OTHER _____

DESCRIBE THE BOOK IN ONE SENTENCE
_____

WHAT DREW ME TO THIS BOOK?
_____

QUOTES/FAVORITE PASSAGES
_____
_____
_____
_____
_____
_____

REVIEW
_____
_____
_____
_____
_____
_____
_____
_____

STARTED BOOK
_____

FINISHED BOOK
_____

WOULD RECOMMEND?
☐ YES   ☐ NO   ☐ MAYBE

RECOMMEND TO
_____

WOULD READ AGAIN?
☐ YES   ☐ NO   ☐ MAYBE

WOULD READ OTHER AUTHOR'S BOOKS?
☐ YES   ☐ NO   ☐ MAYBE

BOOK RATING

EASE OF READING
☆☆☆☆☆

CHARACTERS
☆☆☆☆☆

PLOT
☆☆☆☆☆

ENJOYABILITY
☆☆☆☆☆

OVERALL RATING
☆☆☆☆☆

83

BOOK REVIEW

TITLE	AUTHOR

☐ FICTION   GENRE   FIRST PUBLISHED
☐ NON-FICTION

NEW-TO-ME AUTHOR?   PAGE COUNT   FORMAT ☐ HARDCOVER ☐ PAPERBACK ☐ EBOOK ☐ AUDIOBOOK

☐ YES   ☐ NO   SOURCE ☐ BOUGHT ☐ BORROWED ☐ GIFTED ☐ OTHER _____

STARTED BOOK

FINISHED BOOK

WOULD RECOMMEND?
☐ YES   ☐ NO   ☐ MAYBE

RECOMMEND TO

WOULD READ AGAIN?
☐ YES   ☐ NO   ☐ MAYBE

WOULD READ OTHER AUTHOR'S BOOKS?
☐ YES   ☐ NO   ☐ MAYBE

BOOK RATING

EASE OF READING
☆☆☆☆☆

CHARACTERS
☆☆☆☆☆

PLOT
☆☆☆☆☆

ENJOYABILITY
☆☆☆☆☆

OVERALL RATING
☆☆☆☆☆

DESCRIBE THE BOOK IN ONE SENTENCE

WHAT DREW ME TO THIS BOOK?

QUOTES/FAVORITE PASSAGES

REVIEW

BOOK REVIEW

#

TITLE	AUTHOR

☐ FICTION   GENRE   FIRST PUBLISHED
☐ NON-FICTION   _____   _____

NEW-TO-ME   PAGE   FORMAT ☐ HARDCOVER ☐ PAPERBACK ☐ EBOOK ☐ AUDIOBOOK
AUTHOR?   COUNT

☐   ☐   _____   SOURCE ☐ BOUGHT ☐ BORROWED ☐ GIFTED ☐ OTHER _____
YES   NO

DESCRIBE THE BOOK IN ONE SENTENCE

_____

WHAT DREW ME TO THIS BOOK?

_____

QUOTES/FAVORITE PASSAGES

_____
_____
_____
_____
_____
_____

REVIEW

_____
_____
_____
_____
_____
_____
_____

STARTED BOOK

_____

FINISHED BOOK

_____

WOULD RECOMMEND?
☐ YES   ☐ NO   ☐ MAYBE

RECOMMEND TO

_____

WOULD READ AGAIN?
☐ YES   ☐ NO   ☐ MAYBE

WOULD READ OTHER
AUTHOR'S BOOKS?

☐ YES   ☐ NO   ☐ MAYBE

BOOK RATING

EASE OF READING
☆☆☆☆☆

CHARACTERS
☆☆☆☆☆

PLOT
☆☆☆☆☆

ENJOYABILITY
☆☆☆☆☆

OVERALL RATING
☆☆☆☆☆

BOOK REVIEW

#

TITLE	AUTHOR

☐ FICTION
☐ NON-FICTION

GENRE

_____

FIRST PUBLISHED

_____

NEW-TO-ME AUTHOR?

☐ YES ☐ NO

PAGE COUNT

_____

FORMAT ☐ HARDCOVER ☐ PAPERBACK ☐ EBOOK ☐ AUDIOBOOK

SOURCE ☐ BOUGHT ☐ BORROWED ☐ GIFTED ☐ OTHER _____

STARTED BOOK

_____

FINISHED BOOK

_____

WOULD RECOMMEND?

☐ YES ☐ NO ☐ MAYBE

RECOMMEND TO

_____

WOULD READ AGAIN?

☐ YES ☐ NO ☐ MAYBE

WOULD READ OTHER AUTHOR'S BOOKS?

☐ YES ☐ NO ☐ MAYBE

BOOK RATING

EASE OF READING

☆☆☆☆☆

CHARACTERS

☆☆☆☆☆

PLOT

☆☆☆☆☆

ENJOYABILITY

☆☆☆☆☆

OVERALL RATING

☆☆☆☆☆

DESCRIBE THE BOOK IN ONE SENTENCE

WHAT DREW ME TO THIS BOOK?

QUOTES/FAVORITE PASSAGES

_____
_____
_____
_____
_____

REVIEW

_____
_____
_____
_____
_____
_____
_____
_____

BOOK REVIEW

TITLE	AUTHOR

☐ FICTION   GENRE   FIRST PUBLISHED
☐ NON-FICTION _____ _____

#

NEW-TO-ME   PAGE   FORMAT ☐ HARDCOVER ☐ PAPERBACK ☐ EBOOK ☐ AUDIOBOOK
AUTHOR?   COUNT

☐   ☐   _____   SOURCE ☐ BOUGHT ☐ BORROWED ☐ GIFTED ☐ OTHER _____
YES   NO

DESCRIBE THE BOOK IN ONE SENTENCE
_____

WHAT DREW ME TO THIS BOOK?
_____
_____

QUOTES/FAVORITE PASSAGES
_____
_____
_____
_____
_____
_____
_____

REVIEW
_____
_____
_____
_____
_____
_____
_____
_____

STARTED BOOK
_____

FINISHED BOOK
_____

WOULD RECOMMEND?
☐ YES   ☐ NO   ☐ MAYBE

RECOMMEND TO
_____

WOULD READ AGAIN?
☐ YES   ☐ NO   ☐ MAYBE

WOULD READ OTHER
AUTHOR'S BOOKS?
☐ YES   ☐ NO   ☐ MAYBE

BOOK RATING

EASE OF READING
☆☆☆☆☆

CHARACTERS
☆☆☆☆☆

PLOT
☆☆☆☆☆

ENJOYABILITY
☆☆☆☆☆

OVERALL RATING
☆☆☆☆☆

BOOK REVIEW

#	TITLE	AUTHOR

☐ FICTION   GENRE   FIRST PUBLISHED
☐ NON-FICTION _____   _____

NEW-TO-ME AUTHOR?	PAGE COUNT	FORMAT ☐ HARDCOVER ☐ PAPERBACK ☐ EBOOK ☐ AUDIOBOOK
☐ YES ☐ NO	_____	SOURCE ☐ BOUGHT ☐ BORROWED ☐ GIFTED ☐ OTHER _____

STARTED BOOK

_____

FINISHED BOOK

_____

WOULD RECOMMEND?
☐ YES   ☐ NO   ☐ MAYBE

RECOMMEND TO

_____

WOULD READ AGAIN?
☐ YES   ☐ NO   ☐ MAYBE

WOULD READ OTHER AUTHOR'S BOOKS?

☐ YES   ☐ NO   ☐ MAYBE

BOOK RATING

EASE OF READING
☆☆☆☆☆

CHARACTERS
☆☆☆☆☆

PLOT
☆☆☆☆☆

ENJOYABILITY
☆☆☆☆☆

OVERALL RATING
☆☆☆☆☆

DESCRIBE THE BOOK IN ONE SENTENCE
_____

WHAT DREW ME TO THIS BOOK?
_____

QUOTES/FAVORITE PASSAGES
_____
_____
_____
_____
_____
_____
_____

REVIEW
_____
_____
_____
_____
_____
_____
_____
_____
_____

BOOK REVIEW

#

TITLE	AUTHOR

☐ FICTION   GENRE   FIRST PUBLISHED
☐ NON-FICTION _____ _____

NEW-TO-ME   PAGE   FORMAT ☐ HARDCOVER ☐ PAPERBACK ☐ EBOOK ☐ AUDIOBOOK
AUTHOR?   COUNT
☐   ☐   _____   SOURCE ☐ BOUGHT ☐ BORROWED ☐ GIFTED ☐ OTHER _____
YES   NO

DESCRIBE THE BOOK IN ONE SENTENCE

WHAT DREW ME TO THIS BOOK?

QUOTES/FAVORITE PASSAGES

REVIEW

STARTED BOOK
_____

FINISHED BOOK
_____

WOULD RECOMMEND?
☐ YES   ☐ NO   ☐ MAYBE

RECOMMEND TO
_____

WOULD READ AGAIN?
☐ YES   ☐ NO   ☐ MAYBE

WOULD READ OTHER
AUTHOR'S BOOKS?
☐ YES   ☐ NO   ☐ MAYBE

BOOK RATING

EASE OF READING
☆☆☆☆☆

CHARACTERS
☆☆☆☆☆

PLOT
☆☆☆☆☆

ENJOYABILITY
☆☆☆☆☆

OVERALL RATING
☆☆☆☆☆

BOOK REVIEW

TITLE	AUTHOR

#

☐ FICTION   GENRE   FIRST PUBLISHED
☐ NON-FICTION _____   _____

NEW-TO-ME AUTHOR?   PAGE COUNT

☐ YES   ☐ NO   _____

FORMAT   ☐ HARDCOVER   ☐ PAPERBACK   ☐ EBOOK   ☐ AUDIOBOOK

SOURCE   ☐ BOUGHT   ☐ BORROWED   ☐ GIFTED   ☐ OTHER _____

STARTED BOOK

_____

FINISHED BOOK

_____

WOULD RECOMMEND?

☐ YES   ☐ NO   ☐ MAYBE

RECOMMEND TO

_____

WOULD READ AGAIN?

☐ YES   ☐ NO   ☐ MAYBE

WOULD READ OTHER AUTHOR'S BOOKS?

☐ YES   ☐ NO   ☐ MAYBE

BOOK RATING

EASE OF READING
☆☆☆☆☆

CHARACTERS
☆☆☆☆☆

PLOT
☆☆☆☆☆

ENJOYABILITY
☆☆☆☆☆

OVERALL RATING
☆☆☆☆☆

DESCRIBE THE BOOK IN ONE SENTENCE
_____

WHAT DREW ME TO THIS BOOK?
_____

QUOTES/FAVORITE PASSAGES
_____
_____
_____
_____
_____
_____

REVIEW
_____
_____
_____
_____
_____
_____
_____
_____

BOOK REVIEW

#

TITLE	AUTHOR

☐ FICTION   GENRE   FIRST PUBLISHED
☐ NON-FICTION _____   _____

NEW-TO-ME AUTHOR?   **PAGE COUNT**   FORMAT ☐ HARDCOVER ☐ PAPERBACK ☐ EBOOK ☐ AUDIOBOOK

☐   ☐   _____   SOURCE ☐ BOUGHT ☐ BORROWED ☐ GIFTED ☐ OTHER _____
YES   NO

DESCRIBE THE BOOK IN ONE SENTENCE
_____

WHAT DREW ME TO THIS BOOK?
_____

QUOTES/FAVORITE PASSAGES
_____
_____
_____
_____
_____
_____

REVIEW
_____
_____
_____
_____
_____
_____
_____
_____

STARTED BOOK
_____

FINISHED BOOK
_____

WOULD RECOMMEND?
☐ YES   ☐ NO   ☐ MAYBE
RECOMMEND TO
_____

WOULD READ AGAIN?
☐ YES   ☐ NO   ☐ MAYBE

WOULD READ OTHER AUTHOR'S BOOKS?
☐ YES   ☐ NO   ☐ MAYBE

BOOK RATING

EASE OF READING
☆☆☆☆☆

CHARACTERS
☆☆☆☆☆

PLOT
☆☆☆☆☆

ENJOYABILITY
☆☆☆☆☆

OVERALL RATING
☆☆☆☆☆

BOOK REVIEW

#

TITLE	AUTHOR

☐ FICTION
☐ NON-FICTION

GENRE _____

FIRST PUBLISHED _____

NEW-TO-ME AUTHOR?
☐ YES   ☐ NO

PAGE COUNT
_____

FORMAT ☐ HARDCOVER ☐ PAPERBACK ☐ EBOOK ☐ AUDIOBOOK

SOURCE ☐ BOUGHT ☐ BORROWED ☐ GIFTED ☐ OTHER _____

STARTED BOOK
_____

FINISHED BOOK
_____

WOULD RECOMMEND?
☐ YES   ☐ NO   ☐ MAYBE

RECOMMEND TO
_____

WOULD READ AGAIN?
☐ YES   ☐ NO   ☐ MAYBE

WOULD READ OTHER AUTHOR'S BOOKS?
☐ YES   ☐ NO   ☐ MAYBE

BOOK RATING

EASE OF READING
☆☆☆☆☆

CHARACTERS
☆☆☆☆☆

PLOT
☆☆☆☆☆

ENJOYABILITY
☆☆☆☆☆

OVERALL RATING
☆☆☆☆☆

DESCRIBE THE BOOK IN ONE SENTENCE

WHAT DREW ME TO THIS BOOK?

QUOTES/FAVORITE PASSAGES

REVIEW

BOOK REVIEW

TITLE	AUTHOR

☐ FICTION   GENRE   FIRST PUBLISHED
☐ NON-FICTION _____   _____

NEW-TO-ME AUTHOR?   **PAGE COUNT**   **FORMAT** ☐ HARDCOVER ☐ PAPERBACK ☐ EBOOK ☐ AUDIOBOOK

☐ YES   ☐ NO   _____   **SOURCE** ☐ BOUGHT ☐ BORROWED ☐ GIFTED ☐ OTHER _____

DESCRIBE THE BOOK IN ONE SENTENCE

WHAT DREW ME TO THIS BOOK?

QUOTES/FAVORITE PASSAGES

REVIEW

STARTED BOOK

FINISHED BOOK

WOULD RECOMMEND?
☐ YES   ☐ NO   ☐ MAYBE

RECOMMEND TO

WOULD READ AGAIN?
☐ YES   ☐ NO   ☐ MAYBE

WOULD READ OTHER AUTHOR'S BOOKS?
☐ YES   ☐ NO   ☐ MAYBE

BOOK RATING

EASE OF READING
☆☆☆☆☆

CHARACTERS
☆☆☆☆☆

PLOT
☆☆☆☆☆

ENJOYABILITY
☆☆☆☆☆

OVERALL RATING
☆☆☆☆☆

BOOK REVIEW

TITLE	AUTHOR

☐ FICTION   GENRE   FIRST PUBLISHED
☐ NON-FICTION

NEW-TO-ME AUTHOR?   PAGE COUNT

FORMAT ☐ HARDCOVER ☐ PAPERBACK ☐ EBOOK ☐ AUDIOBOOK

☐ YES ☐ NO

SOURCE ☐ BOUGHT ☐ BORROWED ☐ GIFTED ☐ OTHER _____

STARTED BOOK

FINISHED BOOK

WOULD RECOMMEND?
☐ YES ☐ NO ☐ MAYBE

RECOMMEND TO

WOULD READ AGAIN?
☐ YES ☐ NO ☐ MAYBE

WOULD READ OTHER AUTHOR'S BOOKS?
☐ YES ☐ NO ☐ MAYBE

BOOK RATING

EASE OF READING
☆☆☆☆☆

CHARACTERS
☆☆☆☆☆

PLOT
☆☆☆☆☆

ENJOYABILITY
☆☆☆☆☆

OVERALL RATING
☆☆☆☆☆

DESCRIBE THE BOOK IN ONE SENTENCE

WHAT DREW ME TO THIS BOOK?

QUOTES/FAVORITE PASSAGES

REVIEW

BOOK REVIEW

TITLE	AUTHOR

☐ FICTION   GENRE   FIRST PUBLISHED
☐ NON-FICTION   _____   _____

NEW-TO-ME AUTHOR?   **PAGE COUNT**   **FORMAT** ☐ HARDCOVER ☐ PAPERBACK ☐ EBOOK ☐ AUDIOBOOK

☐ YES   ☐ NO   _____   **SOURCE** ☐ BOUGHT ☐ BORROWED ☐ GIFTED ☐ OTHER _____

DESCRIBE THE BOOK IN ONE SENTENCE

WHAT DREW ME TO THIS BOOK?

QUOTES/FAVORITE PASSAGES

REVIEW

STARTED BOOK

FINISHED BOOK

WOULD RECOMMEND?
☐ YES   ☐ NO   ☐ MAYBE

RECOMMEND TO

WOULD READ AGAIN?
☐ YES   ☐ NO   ☐ MAYBE

WOULD READ OTHER AUTHOR'S BOOKS?
☐ YES   ☐ NO   ☐ MAYBE

BOOK RATING

EASE OF READING
☆☆☆☆☆

CHARACTERS
☆☆☆☆☆

PLOT
☆☆☆☆☆

ENJOYABILITY
☆☆☆☆☆

OVERALL RATING
☆☆☆☆☆

BOOK REVIEW

#

TITLE	AUTHOR

☐ FICTION   GENRE   FIRST PUBLISHED
☐ NON-FICTION   _____   _____

NEW-TO-ME AUTHOR?   **PAGE COUNT**

☐ YES   ☐ NO   _____

FORMAT   ☐ HARDCOVER   ☐ PAPERBACK   ☐ EBOOK   ☐ AUDIOBOOK

SOURCE   ☐ BOUGHT   ☐ BORROWED   ☐ GIFTED   ☐ OTHER _____

STARTED BOOK

_____

FINISHED BOOK

_____

WOULD RECOMMEND?

☐ YES   ☐ NO   ☐ MAYBE

RECOMMEND TO

_____

WOULD READ AGAIN?

☐ YES   ☐ NO   ☐ MAYBE

WOULD READ OTHER AUTHOR'S BOOKS?

☐ YES   ☐ NO   ☐ MAYBE

BOOK RATING

EASE OF READING
☆☆☆☆☆

CHARACTERS
☆☆☆☆☆

PLOT
☆☆☆☆☆

ENJOYABILITY
☆☆☆☆☆

OVERALL RATING
☆☆☆☆☆

DESCRIBE THE BOOK IN ONE SENTENCE

_____

WHAT DREW ME TO THIS BOOK?

_____

QUOTES/FAVORITE PASSAGES

_____

_____

_____

_____

_____

REVIEW

_____

_____

_____

_____

_____

_____

_____

_____

BOOK REVIEW

TITLE	AUTHOR

☐ FICTION   GENRE   FIRST PUBLISHED
☐ NON-FICTION _____ _____

NEW-TO-ME AUTHOR?   PAGE COUNT   FORMAT ☐ HARDCOVER ☐ PAPERBACK ☐ EBOOK ☐ AUDIOBOOK

☐ YES ☐ NO   _____   SOURCE ☐ BOUGHT ☐ BORROWED ☐ GIFTED ☐ OTHER _____

DESCRIBE THE BOOK IN ONE SENTENCE
_____

WHAT DREW ME TO THIS BOOK?
_____

QUOTES/FAVORITE PASSAGES
_____
_____
_____
_____
_____
_____

REVIEW
_____
_____
_____
_____
_____
_____
_____
_____

STARTED BOOK
_____

FINISHED BOOK
_____

WOULD RECOMMEND?
☐ YES   ☐ NO   ☐ MAYBE

RECOMMEND TO
_____

WOULD READ AGAIN?
☐ YES   ☐ NO   ☐ MAYBE

WOULD READ OTHER AUTHOR'S BOOKS?
☐ YES   ☐ NO   ☐ MAYBE

BOOK RATING

EASE OF READING
☆☆☆☆☆

CHARACTERS
☆☆☆☆☆

PLOT
☆☆☆☆☆

ENJOYABILITY
☆☆☆☆☆

OVERALL RATING
☆☆☆☆☆

BOOK REVIEW

#

TITLE	AUTHOR

☐ FICTION　　GENRE　　　　　　　FIRST PUBLISHED
☐ NON-FICTION _____　_____

NEW-TO-ME AUTHOR?　**PAGE COUNT**

FORMAT ☐ HARDCOVER ☐ PAPERBACK ☐ EBOOK ☐ AUDIOBOOK

☐ ☐
YES NO _____

SOURCE ☐ BOUGHT ☐ BORROWED ☐ GIFTED ☐ OTHER _____

STARTED BOOK
_____

FINISHED BOOK
_____

WOULD RECOMMEND?
☐ YES ☐ NO ☐ MAYBE

RECOMMEND TO
_____

WOULD READ AGAIN?
☐ YES ☐ NO ☐ MAYBE

WOULD READ OTHER AUTHOR'S BOOKS?
☐ YES ☐ NO ☐ MAYBE

BOOK RATING

EASE OF READING
☆☆☆☆☆

CHARACTERS
☆☆☆☆☆

PLOT
☆☆☆☆☆

ENJOYABILITY
☆☆☆☆☆

OVERALL RATING
☆☆☆☆☆

DESCRIBE THE BOOK IN ONE SENTENCE
_____

WHAT DREW ME TO THIS BOOK?
_____

QUOTES/FAVORITE PASSAGES
_____
_____
_____
_____
_____
_____

REVIEW
_____
_____
_____
_____
_____
_____
_____
_____

BOOK REVIEW

#

TITLE	AUTHOR

☐ FICTION   GENRE   FIRST PUBLISHED
☐ NON-FICTION _____   _____

NEW-TO-ME   PAGE   FORMAT ☐ HARDCOVER ☐ PAPERBACK ☐ EBOOK ☐ AUDIOBOOK
AUTHOR?   COUNT
☐   ☐   _____   SOURCE ☐ BOUGHT ☐ BORROWED ☐ GIFTED ☐ OTHER _____
YES   NO

DESCRIBE THE BOOK IN ONE SENTENCE
_____

WHAT DREW ME TO THIS BOOK?
_____

QUOTES/FAVORITE PASSAGES
_____
_____
_____
_____
_____
_____

REVIEW
_____
_____
_____
_____
_____
_____
_____
_____

STARTED BOOK
_____

FINISHED BOOK
_____

WOULD RECOMMEND?
☐ YES   ☐ NO   ☐ MAYBE
RECOMMEND TO
_____

WOULD READ AGAIN?
☐ YES   ☐ NO   ☐ MAYBE

WOULD READ OTHER
AUTHOR'S BOOKS?
☐ YES   ☐ NO   ☐ MAYBE

BOOK RATING
EASE OF READING
☆☆☆☆☆
CHARACTERS
☆☆☆☆☆
PLOT
☆☆☆☆☆
ENJOYABILITY
☆☆☆☆☆

OVERALL RATING
☆☆☆☆☆

BOOK REVIEW

TITLE	AUTHOR

☐ FICTION   GENRE   FIRST PUBLISHED
☐ NON-FICTION _____ _____

NEW-TO-ME AUTHOR?   **PAGE COUNT**

☐ YES   ☐ NO   _____

FORMAT   ☐ HARDCOVER ☐ PAPERBACK ☐ EBOOK ☐ AUDIOBOOK

SOURCE   ☐ BOUGHT ☐ BORROWED ☐ GIFTED ☐ OTHER _____

STARTED BOOK

_____

FINISHED BOOK

_____

WOULD RECOMMEND?

☐ YES   ☐ NO   ☐ MAYBE

RECOMMEND TO

_____

WOULD READ AGAIN?

☐ YES   ☐ NO   ☐ MAYBE

WOULD READ OTHER AUTHOR'S BOOKS?

☐ YES   ☐ NO   ☐ MAYBE

BOOK RATING

EASE OF READING
☆☆☆☆☆

CHARACTERS
☆☆☆☆☆

PLOT
☆☆☆☆☆

ENJOYABILITY
☆☆☆☆☆

OVERALL RATING
☆☆☆☆☆

DESCRIBE THE BOOK IN ONE SENTENCE
_____

WHAT DREW ME TO THIS BOOK?
_____

QUOTES/FAVORITE PASSAGES
_____
_____
_____
_____
_____
_____

REVIEW
_____
_____
_____
_____
_____
_____
_____
_____

BOOK REVIEW

#

TITLE	AUTHOR

☐ FICTION   GENRE   FIRST PUBLISHED
☐ NON-FICTION _____ _____

NEW-TO-ME   PAGE   FORMAT ☐ HARDCOVER ☐ PAPERBACK ☐ EBOOK ☐ AUDIOBOOK
AUTHOR?   COUNT
☐   ☐   _____   SOURCE ☐ BOUGHT ☐ BORROWED ☐ GIFTED ☐ OTHER _____
YES NO

DESCRIBE THE BOOK IN ONE SENTENCE

WHAT DREW ME TO THIS BOOK?

QUOTES/FAVORITE PASSAGES

REVIEW

STARTED BOOK

FINISHED BOOK

WOULD RECOMMEND?
☐ YES   ☐ NO   ☐ MAYBE
RECOMMEND TO

WOULD READ AGAIN?
☐ YES   ☐ NO   ☐ MAYBE

WOULD READ OTHER
AUTHOR'S BOOKS?
☐ YES   ☐ NO   ☐ MAYBE

BOOK RATING
EASE OF READING
☆☆☆☆☆
CHARACTERS
☆☆☆☆☆
PLOT
☆☆☆☆☆
ENJOYABILITY
☆☆☆☆☆
OVERALL RATING
☆☆☆☆☆

BOOK REVIEW

#

TITLE	AUTHOR

☐ FICTION GENRE FIRST PUBLISHED
☐ NON-FICTION _____ _____

NEW-TO-ME AUTHOR? PAGE COUNT FORMAT ☐ HARDCOVER ☐ PAPERBACK ☐ EBOOK ☐ AUDIOBOOK

☐ YES ☐ NO _____ SOURCE ☐ BOUGHT ☐ BORROWED ☐ GIFTED ☐ OTHER _____

STARTED BOOK

_____

FINISHED BOOK

_____

WOULD RECOMMEND?
☐ YES ☐ NO ☐ MAYBE
RECOMMEND TO

_____

WOULD READ AGAIN?
☐ YES ☐ NO ☐ MAYBE

WOULD READ OTHER AUTHOR'S BOOKS?
☐ YES ☐ NO ☐ MAYBE

BOOK RATING

EASE OF READING
☆☆☆☆☆

CHARACTERS
☆☆☆☆☆

PLOT
☆☆☆☆☆

ENJOYABILITY
☆☆☆☆☆

OVERALL RATING
☆☆☆☆☆

DESCRIBE THE BOOK IN ONE SENTENCE
_____

WHAT DREW ME TO THIS BOOK?
_____

QUOTES/FAVORITE PASSAGES
_____
_____
_____
_____
_____
_____
_____

REVIEW
_____
_____
_____
_____
_____
_____
_____
_____
_____

BOOK REVIEW

#

TITLE	AUTHOR

☐ FICTION   GENRE   FIRST PUBLISHED
☐ NON-FICTION   _____   _____

NEW-TO-ME   PAGE   FORMAT ☐ HARDCOVER ☐ PAPERBACK ☐ EBOOK ☐ AUDIOBOOK
AUTHOR?   COUNT

☐   ☐   _____   SOURCE ☐ BOUGHT ☐ BORROWED ☐ GIFTED ☐ OTHER _____
YES   NO

DESCRIBE THE BOOK IN ONE SENTENCE
_____

WHAT DREW ME TO THIS BOOK?
_____

QUOTES/FAVORITE PASSAGES
_____
_____
_____
_____
_____
_____

REVIEW
_____
_____
_____
_____
_____
_____
_____

STARTED BOOK
_____

FINISHED BOOK
_____

WOULD RECOMMEND?
☐ YES   ☐ NO   ☐ MAYBE
RECOMMEND TO
_____

WOULD READ AGAIN?
☐ YES   ☐ NO   ☐ MAYBE

WOULD READ OTHER
AUTHOR'S BOOKS?
☐ YES   ☐ NO   ☐ MAYBE

BOOK RATING
EASE OF READING
☆☆☆☆☆
CHARACTERS
☆☆☆☆☆
PLOT
☆☆☆☆☆
ENJOYABILITY
☆☆☆☆☆

OVERALL RATING
☆☆☆☆☆

BOOK REVIEW

#

TITLE	AUTHOR

☐ FICTION GENRE FIRST PUBLISHED
☐ NON-FICTION _____ _____

NEW-TO-ME AUTHOR? **PAGE COUNT**

☐ ☐
YES NO

_____

FORMAT ☐ HARDCOVER ☐ PAPERBACK ☐ EBOOK ☐ AUDIOBOOK

SOURCE ☐ BOUGHT ☐ BORROWED ☐ GIFTED ☐ OTHER _____

STARTED BOOK

_____

FINISHED BOOK

_____

WOULD RECOMMEND?
☐ YES ☐ NO ☐ MAYBE

RECOMMEND TO

_____

WOULD READ AGAIN?
☐ YES ☐ NO ☐ MAYBE

WOULD READ OTHER AUTHOR'S BOOKS?

☐ YES ☐ NO ☐ MAYBE

BOOK RATING

EASE OF READING
☆☆☆☆☆

CHARACTERS
☆☆☆☆☆

PLOT
☆☆☆☆☆

ENJOYABILITY
☆☆☆☆☆

OVERALL RATING
☆☆☆☆☆

DESCRIBE THE BOOK IN ONE SENTENCE
_____

WHAT DREW ME TO THIS BOOK?
_____

QUOTES/FAVORITE PASSAGES
_____
_____
_____
_____
_____
_____

REVIEW
_____
_____
_____
_____
_____
_____
_____
_____

BOOK REVIEW

____

TITLE	AUTHOR

☐ FICTION   GENRE   FIRST PUBLISHED
☐ NON-FICTION   _____   _____

NEW-TO-ME AUTHOR?   PAGE COUNT   FORMAT ☐ HARDCOVER ☐ PAPERBACK ☐ EBOOK ☐ AUDIOBOOK

☐ YES   ☐ NO   _____   SOURCE ☐ BOUGHT ☐ BORROWED ☐ GIFTED ☐ OTHER _____

DESCRIBE THE BOOK IN ONE SENTENCE
_____

WHAT DREW ME TO THIS BOOK?
_____

QUOTES/FAVORITE PASSAGES
_____
_____
_____
_____
_____
_____

REVIEW
_____
_____
_____
_____
_____
_____
_____
_____

STARTED BOOK
_____

FINISHED BOOK
_____

WOULD RECOMMEND?
☐ YES   ☐ NO   ☐ MAYBE

RECOMMEND TO
_____

WOULD READ AGAIN?
☐ YES   ☐ NO   ☐ MAYBE

WOULD READ OTHER AUTHOR'S BOOKS?
☐ YES   ☐ NO   ☐ MAYBE

BOOK RATING

EASE OF READING
☆☆☆☆☆

CHARACTERS
☆☆☆☆☆

PLOT
☆☆☆☆☆

ENJOYABILITY
☆☆☆☆☆

OVERALL RATING
☆☆☆☆☆

SERIES REVIEWS

SERIES REVIEWS

SERIES REVIEW

	TITLE	AUTHOR
#		

☐ FICTION   GENRE   PUBLICATION DATES
☐ NON-FICTION   _____   _____

BOOKS IN SERIES   **SERIES COMPLETE?**   **FORMAT** ☐ HARDCOVER ☐ PAPERBACK ☐ EBOOK ☐ AUDIOBOOK

_____   ☐ YES ☐ NO   **SOURCE** ☐ BOUGHT ☐ BORROWED ☐ GIFTED ☐ OTHER _____

STARTED SERIES

_____

FINISHED SERIES

_____

WOULD RECOMMEND?
☐ YES ☐ NO ☐ MAYBE
RECOMMEND TO

_____

WOULD READ AGAIN?
☐ YES ☐ NO ☐ MAYBE

WOULD READ OTHER AUTHOR'S BOOKS?

☐ YES ☐ NO ☐ MAYBE

SERIES RATING

EASE OF READING
☆☆☆☆☆

CHARACTERS
☆☆☆☆☆

PLOT
☆☆☆☆☆

ENJOYABILITY
☆☆☆☆☆

OVERALL RATING
☆☆☆☆☆

DESCRIBE THE SERIES IN ONE SENTENCE

WHAT DREW ME TO THIS SERIES?

QUOTES/FAVORITE PASSAGES

REVIEW

SERIES REVIEW

#

TITLE	AUTHOR

☐ FICTION   GENRE   FIRST PUBLISHED
☐ NON-FICTION   _____ _____

BOOKS IN SERIES   SERIES COMPLETE?   FORMAT ☐ HARDCOVER ☐ PAPERBACK ☐ EBOOK ☐ AUDIOBOOK

_____   ☐   ☐   SOURCE ☐ BOUGHT ☐ BORROWED ☐ GIFTED ☐ OTHER _____
                YES   NO

DESCRIBE THE SERIES IN ONE SENTENCE
_____

WHAT DREW ME TO THIS SERIES?
_____

QUOTES/FAVORITE PASSAGES
_____
_____
_____
_____
_____
_____

REVIEW
_____
_____
_____
_____
_____
_____
_____
_____
_____
_____

STARTED SERIES
_____

FINISHED SERIES
_____

WOULD RECOMMEND?
☐ YES   ☐ NO   ☐ MAYBE
RECOMMEND TO
_____

WOULD READ AGAIN?
☐ YES   ☐ NO   ☐ MAYBE

WOULD READ OTHER AUTHOR'S WORKS?
☐ YES   ☐ NO   ☐ MAYBE

SERIES RATING
EASE OF READING
☆☆☆☆☆
CHARACTERS
☆☆☆☆☆
PLOT
☆☆☆☆☆
ENJOYABILITY
☆☆☆☆☆

OVERALL RATING
☆☆☆☆☆

SERIES REVIEW

TITLE	AUTHOR

#

☐ FICTION   GENRE   PUBLICATION DATES
☐ NON-FICTION

BOOKS IN SERIES   SERIES COMPLETE?

FORMAT   ☐ HARDCOVER   ☐ PAPERBACK   ☐ EBOOK   ☐ AUDIOBOOK

☐ YES   ☐ NO

SOURCE   ☐ BOUGHT   ☐ BORROWED   ☐ GIFTED   ☐ OTHER _____

STARTED SERIES

FINISHED SERIES

WOULD RECOMMEND?
☐ YES   ☐ NO   ☐ MAYBE

RECOMMEND TO

WOULD READ AGAIN?
☐ YES   ☐ NO   ☐ MAYBE

WOULD READ OTHER AUTHOR'S BOOKS?
☐ YES   ☐ NO   ☐ MAYBE

SERIES RATING

EASE OF READING
☆☆☆☆☆

CHARACTERS
☆☆☆☆☆

PLOT
☆☆☆☆☆

ENJOYABILITY
☆☆☆☆☆

OVERALL RATING
☆☆☆☆☆

DESCRIBE THE SERIES IN ONE SENTENCE

WHAT DREW ME TO THIS SERIES?

QUOTES/FAVORITE PASSAGES

REVIEW

SERIES REVIEW

TITLE	AUTHOR

#

☐ FICTION
☐ NON-FICTION

GENRE

FIRST PUBLISHED

BOOKS IN SERIES

SERIES COMPLETE?
☐ YES ☐ NO

FORMAT ☐ HARDCOVER ☐ PAPERBACK ☐ EBOOK ☐ AUDIOBOOK

SOURCE ☐ BOUGHT ☐ BORROWED ☐ GIFTED ☐ OTHER _____

DESCRIBE THE SERIES IN ONE SENTENCE

WHAT DREW ME TO THIS SERIES?

QUOTES/FAVORITE PASSAGES

REVIEW

STARTED SERIES

FINISHED SERIES

WOULD RECOMMEND?
☐ YES ☐ NO ☐ MAYBE

RECOMMEND TO

WOULD READ AGAIN?
☐ YES ☐ NO ☐ MAYBE

WOULD READ OTHER AUTHOR'S WORKS?
☐ YES ☐ NO ☐ MAYBE

SERIES RATING

EASE OF READING
☆☆☆☆☆

CHARACTERS
☆☆☆☆☆

PLOT
☆☆☆☆☆

ENJOYABILITY
☆☆☆☆☆

OVERALL RATING
☆☆☆☆☆

SERIES REVIEW

___

TITLE	AUTHOR

☐ FICTION
☐ NON-FICTION

GENRE ___

PUBLICATION DATES ___

BOOKS IN SERIES ___

SERIES COMPLETE?
☐ YES ☐ NO

FORMAT ☐ HARDCOVER ☐ PAPERBACK ☐ EBOOK ☐ AUDIOBOOK

SOURCE ☐ BOUGHT ☐ BORROWED ☐ GIFTED ☐ OTHER ___

STARTED SERIES
___

FINISHED SERIES
___

WOULD RECOMMEND?
☐ YES ☐ NO ☐ MAYBE

RECOMMEND TO
___

WOULD READ AGAIN?
☐ YES ☐ NO ☐ MAYBE

WOULD READ OTHER AUTHOR'S BOOKS?
☐ YES ☐ NO ☐ MAYBE

SERIES RATING

EASE OF READING
☆☆☆☆☆

CHARACTERS
☆☆☆☆☆

PLOT
☆☆☆☆☆

ENJOYABILITY
☆☆☆☆☆

OVERALL RATING
☆☆☆☆☆

DESCRIBE THE SERIES IN ONE SENTENCE
___

WHAT DREW ME TO THIS SERIES?
___

QUOTES/FAVORITE PASSAGES
___
___
___
___
___
___
___

REVIEW
___
___
___
___
___
___
___
___
___
___

SERIES REVIEW

TITLE	AUTHOR

#

☐ FICTION   GENRE   FIRST PUBLISHED
☐ NON-FICTION _____ _____

BOOKS IN   SERIES   FORMAT ☐ HARDCOVER ☐ PAPERBACK ☐ EBOOK ☐ AUDIOBOOK
SERIES   COMPLETE?

_____   ☐   ☐   SOURCE ☐ BOUGHT ☐ BORROWED ☐ GIFTED ☐ OTHER _____
        YES   NO

DESCRIBE THE SERIES IN ONE SENTENCE

_____

WHAT DREW ME TO THIS SERIES?

_____

QUOTES/FAVORITE PASSAGES

_____

_____

_____

_____

_____

_____

REVIEW

_____

_____

_____

_____

_____

_____

_____

_____

STARTED SERIES

_____

FINISHED SERIES

_____

WOULD RECOMMEND?

☐ YES   ☐ NO   ☐ MAYBE

RECOMMEND TO

_____

WOULD READ AGAIN?

☐ YES   ☐ NO   ☐ MAYBE

WOULD READ OTHER
AUTHOR'S WORKS?

☐ YES   ☐ NO   ☐ MAYBE

SERIES RATING

EASE OF READING

☆☆☆☆☆

CHARACTERS

☆☆☆☆☆

PLOT

☆☆☆☆☆

ENJOYABILITY

☆☆☆☆☆

OVERALL RATING

☆☆☆☆☆

SERIES REVIEW

#	TITLE	AUTHOR

☐ FICTION   GENRE   PUBLICATION DATES
☐ NON-FICTION

BOOKS IN SERIES   **SERIES COMPLETE?**   **FORMAT** ☐ HARDCOVER ☐ PAPERBACK ☐ EBOOK ☐ AUDIOBOOK

_____   ☐ YES   ☐ NO   **SOURCE** ☐ BOUGHT ☐ BORROWED ☐ GIFTED ☐ OTHER _____

STARTED SERIES

_____

FINISHED SERIES

_____

WOULD RECOMMEND?
☐ YES   ☐ NO   ☐ MAYBE

RECOMMEND TO

_____

WOULD READ AGAIN?
☐ YES   ☐ NO   ☐ MAYBE

WOULD READ OTHER AUTHOR'S BOOKS?

☐ YES   ☐ NO   ☐ MAYBE

SERIES RATING

EASE OF READING
☆☆☆☆☆

CHARACTERS
☆☆☆☆☆

PLOT
☆☆☆☆☆

ENJOYABILITY
☆☆☆☆☆

OVERALL RATING
☆☆☆☆☆

DESCRIBE THE SERIES IN ONE SENTENCE

_____

WHAT DREW ME TO THIS SERIES?

_____

QUOTES/FAVORITE PASSAGES

_____
_____
_____
_____
_____
_____

REVIEW

_____
_____
_____
_____
_____
_____
_____
_____

SERIES REVIEW

TITLE	AUTHOR

#

☐ FICTION   GENRE   FIRST PUBLISHED
☐ NON-FICTION   _____   _____

BOOKS IN SERIES   **SERIES COMPLETE?**   **FORMAT** ☐ HARDCOVER ☐ PAPERBACK ☐ EBOOK ☐ AUDIOBOOK

_____   ☐ YES ☐ NO   **SOURCE** ☐ BOUGHT ☐ BORROWED ☐ GIFTED ☐ OTHER _____

DESCRIBE THE SERIES IN ONE SENTENCE
_____

WHAT DREW ME TO THIS SERIES?
_____

QUOTES/FAVORITE PASSAGES
_____
_____
_____
_____
_____
_____

REVIEW
_____
_____
_____
_____
_____
_____
_____
_____
_____

STARTED SERIES
_____

FINISHED SERIES
_____

WOULD RECOMMEND?
☐ YES   ☐ NO   ☐ MAYBE
RECOMMEND TO
_____

WOULD READ AGAIN?
☐ YES   ☐ NO   ☐ MAYBE

WOULD READ OTHER AUTHOR'S WORKS?
☐ YES   ☐ NO   ☐ MAYBE

SERIES RATING

EASE OF READING
☆☆☆☆☆

CHARACTERS
☆☆☆☆☆

PLOT
☆☆☆☆☆

ENJOYABILITY
☆☆☆☆☆

OVERALL RATING
☆☆☆☆☆

115

SERIES REVIEW

TITLE	AUTHOR

#

☐ FICTION
☐ NON-FICTION

GENRE _____

PUBLICATION DATES _____

BOOKS IN SERIES

SERIES COMPLETE?
☐ YES ☐ NO

_____

FORMAT ☐ HARDCOVER ☐ PAPERBACK ☐ EBOOK ☐ AUDIOBOOK

SOURCE ☐ BOUGHT ☐ BORROWED ☐ GIFTED ☐ OTHER _____

STARTED SERIES
_____

FINISHED SERIES
_____

WOULD RECOMMEND?
☐ YES   ☐ NO   ☐ MAYBE

RECOMMEND TO
_____

WOULD READ AGAIN?
☐ YES   ☐ NO   ☐ MAYBE

WOULD READ OTHER AUTHOR'S BOOKS?
☐ YES   ☐ NO   ☐ MAYBE

SERIES RATING

EASE OF READING
☆☆☆☆☆

CHARACTERS
☆☆☆☆☆

PLOT
☆☆☆☆☆

ENJOYABILITY
☆☆☆☆☆

OVERALL RATING
☆☆☆☆☆

DESCRIBE THE SERIES IN ONE SENTENCE
_____

WHAT DREW ME TO THIS SERIES?
_____

QUOTES/FAVORITE PASSAGES
_____
_____
_____
_____
_____
_____

REVIEW
_____
_____
_____
_____
_____
_____
_____
_____
_____

116

SERIES REVIEW

#	TITLE	AUTHOR

☐ FICTION   GENRE   FIRST PUBLISHED
☐ NON-FICTION _____   _____

BOOKS IN SERIES   SERIES COMPLETE?   FORMAT ☐ HARDCOVER ☐ PAPERBACK ☐ EBOOK ☐ AUDIOBOOK

_____   ☐ YES   ☐ NO   SOURCE ☐ BOUGHT ☐ BORROWED ☐ GIFTED ☐ OTHER _____

DESCRIBE THE SERIES IN ONE SENTENCE

_____

WHAT DREW ME TO THIS SERIES?

_____

QUOTES/FAVORITE PASSAGES

_____
_____
_____
_____
_____
_____

REVIEW

_____
_____
_____
_____
_____
_____
_____
_____

STARTED SERIES

_____

FINISHED SERIES

_____

WOULD RECOMMEND?
☐ YES   ☐ NO   ☐ MAYBE

RECOMMEND TO

_____

WOULD READ AGAIN?
☐ YES   ☐ NO   ☐ MAYBE

WOULD READ OTHER AUTHOR'S WORKS?
☐ YES   ☐ NO   ☐ MAYBE

SERIES RATING

EASE OF READING
☆☆☆☆☆

CHARACTERS
☆☆☆☆☆

PLOT
☆☆☆☆☆

ENJOYABILITY
☆☆☆☆☆

OVERALL RATING
☆☆☆☆☆

SERIES REVIEW

TITLE	AUTHOR

#

☐ FICTION   GENRE   PUBLICATION DATES
☐ NON-FICTION _____   _____

BOOKS IN SERIES   **SERIES COMPLETE?**

_____   ☐ YES ☐ NO

FORMAT ☐ HARDCOVER ☐ PAPERBACK ☐ EBOOK ☐ AUDIOBOOK

SOURCE ☐ BOUGHT ☐ BORROWED ☐ GIFTED ☐ OTHER _____

STARTED SERIES

_____

FINISHED SERIES

_____

WOULD RECOMMEND?
☐ YES ☐ NO ☐ MAYBE

RECOMMEND TO

_____

WOULD READ AGAIN?
☐ YES ☐ NO ☐ MAYBE

WOULD READ OTHER AUTHOR'S BOOKS?

☐ YES ☐ NO ☐ MAYBE

SERIES RATING

EASE OF READING
☆☆☆☆☆

CHARACTERS
☆☆☆☆☆

PLOT
☆☆☆☆☆

ENJOYABILITY
☆☆☆☆☆

OVERALL RATING
☆☆☆☆☆

DESCRIBE THE SERIES IN ONE SENTENCE
_____

WHAT DREW ME TO THIS SERIES?
_____

QUOTES/FAVORITE PASSAGES
_____
_____
_____
_____
_____
_____

REVIEW
_____
_____
_____
_____
_____
_____
_____
_____
_____

SERIES REVIEW

TITLE	AUTHOR

#

☐ FICTION   GENRE   FIRST PUBLISHED
☐ NON-FICTION _____ _____

BOOKS IN SERIES   SERIES COMPLETE?   FORMAT ☐ HARDCOVER ☐ PAPERBACK ☐ EBOOK ☐ AUDIOBOOK

_____   ☐ YES   ☐ NO   SOURCE ☐ BOUGHT ☐ BORROWED ☐ GIFTED ☐ OTHER _____

DESCRIBE THE SERIES IN ONE SENTENCE
_____

WHAT DREW ME TO THIS SERIES?
_____

QUOTES/FAVORITE PASSAGES
_____
_____
_____
_____
_____
_____

REVIEW
_____
_____
_____
_____
_____
_____
_____
_____

STARTED SERIES
_____

FINISHED SERIES
_____

WOULD RECOMMEND?
☐ YES   ☐ NO   ☐ MAYBE

RECOMMEND TO
_____

WOULD READ AGAIN?
☐ YES   ☐ NO   ☐ MAYBE

WOULD READ OTHER AUTHOR'S WORKS?
☐ YES   ☐ NO   ☐ MAYBE

SERIES RATING

EASE OF READING
☆☆☆☆☆

CHARACTERS
☆☆☆☆☆

PLOT
☆☆☆☆☆

ENJOYABILITY
☆☆☆☆☆

OVERALL RATING
☆☆☆☆☆

SERIES REVIEW

TITLE	AUTHOR

#

☐ FICTION
☐ NON-FICTION

GENRE

PUBLICATION DATES

BOOKS IN SERIES

SERIES COMPLETE?

☐ YES ☐ NO

FORMAT ☐ HARDCOVER ☐ PAPERBACK ☐ EBOOK ☐ AUDIOBOOK

SOURCE ☐ BOUGHT ☐ BORROWED ☐ GIFTED ☐ OTHER _____

STARTED SERIES

FINISHED SERIES

WOULD RECOMMEND?
☐ YES ☐ NO ☐ MAYBE

RECOMMEND TO

WOULD READ AGAIN?
☐ YES ☐ NO ☐ MAYBE

WOULD READ OTHER AUTHOR'S BOOKS?
☐ YES ☐ NO ☐ MAYBE

SERIES RATING

EASE OF READING
☆☆☆☆☆

CHARACTERS
☆☆☆☆☆

PLOT
☆☆☆☆☆

ENJOYABILITY
☆☆☆☆☆

OVERALL RATING
☆☆☆☆☆

DESCRIBE THE SERIES IN ONE SENTENCE

WHAT DREW ME TO THIS SERIES?

QUOTES/FAVORITE PASSAGES

REVIEW

SERIES REVIEW

#	

TITLE	AUTHOR

☐ FICTION   GENRE   FIRST PUBLISHED
☐ NON-FICTION   _____   _____

BOOKS IN SERIES   **SERIES COMPLETE?**   **FORMAT** ☐ HARDCOVER ☐ PAPERBACK ☐ EBOOK ☐ AUDIOBOOK

_____   ☐   ☐   **SOURCE** ☐ BOUGHT ☐ BORROWED ☐ GIFTED ☐ OTHER _____
             YES   NO

DESCRIBE THE SERIES IN ONE SENTENCE
_____

WHAT DREW ME TO THIS SERIES?
_____

QUOTES/FAVORITE PASSAGES
_____
_____
_____
_____
_____
_____

REVIEW
_____
_____
_____
_____
_____
_____
_____
_____

STARTED SERIES
_____

FINISHED SERIES
_____

WOULD RECOMMEND?
☐ YES   ☐ NO   ☐ MAYBE
RECOMMEND TO
_____

WOULD READ AGAIN?
☐ YES   ☐ NO   ☐ MAYBE

WOULD READ OTHER AUTHOR'S WORKS?
☐ YES   ☐ NO   ☐ MAYBE

SERIES RATING

EASE OF READING
☆☆☆☆☆

CHARACTERS
☆☆☆☆☆

PLOT
☆☆☆☆☆

ENJOYABILITY
☆☆☆☆☆

OVERALL RATING
☆☆☆☆☆

SERIES REVIEW

TITLE	AUTHOR

#

☐ FICTION
☐ NON-FICTION

GENRE
_____

PUBLICATION DATES
_____

BOOKS IN SERIES

SERIES COMPLETE?
☐ YES ☐ NO

FORMAT ☐ HARDCOVER ☐ PAPERBACK ☐ EBOOK ☐ AUDIOBOOK

SOURCE ☐ BOUGHT ☐ BORROWED ☐ GIFTED ☐ OTHER _____

STARTED SERIES
_____

FINISHED SERIES
_____

WOULD RECOMMEND?
☐ YES ☐ NO ☐ MAYBE

RECOMMEND TO
_____

WOULD READ AGAIN?
☐ YES ☐ NO ☐ MAYBE

WOULD READ OTHER AUTHOR'S BOOKS?
☐ YES ☐ NO ☐ MAYBE

SERIES RATING

EASE OF READING
☆☆☆☆☆

CHARACTERS
☆☆☆☆☆

PLOT
☆☆☆☆☆

ENJOYABILITY
☆☆☆☆☆

OVERALL RATING
☆☆☆☆☆

DESCRIBE THE SERIES IN ONE SENTENCE
_____

WHAT DREW ME TO THIS SERIES?
_____

QUOTES/FAVORITE PASSAGES
_____
_____
_____
_____
_____
_____
_____

REVIEW
_____
_____
_____
_____
_____
_____
_____
_____
_____
_____

SERIES REVIEW

	TITLE	AUTHOR
#		

☐ FICTION   GENRE   FIRST PUBLISHED
☐ NON-FICTION

BOOKS IN   SERIES   FORMAT ☐ HARDCOVER ☐ PAPERBACK ☐ EBOOK ☐ AUDIOBOOK
SERIES   COMPLETE?

☐   ☐   SOURCE ☐ BOUGHT ☐ BORROWED ☐ GIFTED ☐ OTHER _____
YES   NO

DESCRIBE THE SERIES IN ONE SENTENCE

WHAT DREW ME TO THIS SERIES?

QUOTES/FAVORITE PASSAGES

REVIEW

STARTED SERIES

FINISHED SERIES

WOULD RECOMMEND?
☐ YES   ☐ NO   ☐ MAYBE

RECOMMEND TO

WOULD READ AGAIN?
☐ YES   ☐ NO   ☐ MAYBE

WOULD READ OTHER
AUTHOR'S WORKS?
☐ YES   ☐ NO   ☐ MAYBE

SERIES RATING

EASE OF READING
☆☆☆☆☆

CHARACTERS
☆☆☆☆☆

PLOT
☆☆☆☆☆

ENJOYABILITY
☆☆☆☆☆

OVERALL RATING
☆☆☆☆☆

123

SERIES REVIEW

#	TITLE	AUTHOR

☐ FICTION
☐ NON-FICTION

GENRE _____

PUBLICATION DATES _____

BOOKS IN SERIES
_____

SERIES COMPLETE?
☐ YES ☐ NO

FORMAT ☐ HARDCOVER ☐ PAPERBACK ☐ EBOOK ☐ AUDIOBOOK

SOURCE ☐ BOUGHT ☐ BORROWED ☐ GIFTED ☐ OTHER _____

STARTED SERIES
_____

FINISHED SERIES
_____

WOULD RECOMMEND?
☐ YES ☐ NO ☐ MAYBE

RECOMMEND TO
_____

WOULD READ AGAIN?
☐ YES ☐ NO ☐ MAYBE

WOULD READ OTHER AUTHOR'S BOOKS?
☐ YES ☐ NO ☐ MAYBE

SERIES RATING

EASE OF READING
☆☆☆☆☆

CHARACTERS
☆☆☆☆☆

PLOT
☆☆☆☆☆

ENJOYABILITY
☆☆☆☆☆

OVERALL RATING
☆☆☆☆☆

DESCRIBE THE SERIES IN ONE SENTENCE
_____

WHAT DREW ME TO THIS SERIES?
_____

QUOTES/FAVORITE PASSAGES
_____
_____
_____
_____
_____
_____

REVIEW
_____
_____
_____
_____
_____
_____
_____
_____

SERIES REVIEW

___

TITLE	AUTHOR

☐ FICTION   GENRE   FIRST PUBLISHED
☐ NON-FICTION   _____   _____

BOOKS IN   SERIES   FORMAT ☐ HARDCOVER ☐ PAPERBACK ☐ EBOOK ☐ AUDIOBOOK
SERIES   COMPLETE?

_____   ☐   ☐   SOURCE ☐ BOUGHT ☐ BORROWED ☐ GIFTED ☐ OTHER _____
        YES   NO

DESCRIBE THE SERIES IN ONE SENTENCE
_____

WHAT DREW ME TO THIS SERIES?
_____

QUOTES/FAVORITE PASSAGES
_____
_____
_____
_____
_____
_____

REVIEW
_____
_____
_____
_____
_____
_____
_____
_____
_____

STARTED SERIES
_____

FINISHED SERIES
_____

WOULD RECOMMEND?
☐ YES   ☐ NO   ☐ MAYBE

RECOMMEND TO
_____

WOULD READ AGAIN?
☐ YES   ☐ NO   ☐ MAYBE

WOULD READ OTHER AUTHOR'S WORKS?
☐ YES   ☐ NO   ☐ MAYBE

SERIES RATING

EASE OF READING
☆☆☆☆☆

CHARACTERS
☆☆☆☆☆

PLOT
☆☆☆☆☆

ENJOYABILITY
☆☆☆☆☆

OVERALL RATING
☆☆☆☆☆

SERIES REVIEW

#	TITLE	AUTHOR

☐ FICTION　　GENRE　　　　　　PUBLICATION DATES
☐ NON-FICTION　_____　_____　_____

BOOKS IN SERIES　SERIES COMPLETE?

FORMAT　☐ HARDCOVER　☐ PAPERBACK　☐ EBOOK　☐ AUDIOBOOK

_____　☐ YES　☐ NO

SOURCE　☐ BOUGHT　☐ BORROWED　☐ GIFTED　☐ OTHER _____

STARTED SERIES
_____

FINISHED SERIES
_____

WOULD RECOMMEND?
☐ YES　☐ NO　☐ MAYBE

RECOMMEND TO
_____

WOULD READ AGAIN?
☐ YES　☐ NO　☐ MAYBE

WOULD READ OTHER AUTHOR'S BOOKS?
☐ YES　☐ NO　☐ MAYBE

SERIES RATING

EASE OF READING
☆☆☆☆☆

CHARACTERS
☆☆☆☆☆

PLOT
☆☆☆☆☆

ENJOYABILITY
☆☆☆☆☆

OVERALL RATING
☆☆☆☆☆

DESCRIBE THE SERIES IN ONE SENTENCE
_____

WHAT DREW ME TO THIS SERIES?
_____

QUOTES/FAVORITE PASSAGES
_____
_____
_____
_____
_____
_____

REVIEW
_____
_____
_____
_____
_____
_____
_____
_____
_____
_____

SERIES REVIEW

TITLE	AUTHOR

#

☐ FICTION   GENRE   FIRST PUBLISHED
☐ NON-FICTION _____ _____

BOOKS IN SERIES
_____

SERIES COMPLETE?
☐ YES ☐ NO

FORMAT ☐ HARDCOVER ☐ PAPERBACK ☐ EBOOK ☐ AUDIOBOOK

SOURCE ☐ BOUGHT ☐ BORROWED ☐ GIFTED ☐ OTHER _____

DESCRIBE THE SERIES IN ONE SENTENCE
_____

WHAT DREW ME TO THIS SERIES?
_____

QUOTES/FAVORITE PASSAGES
_____
_____
_____
_____
_____
_____

REVIEW
_____
_____
_____
_____
_____
_____
_____
_____
_____

STARTED SERIES
_____

FINISHED SERIES
_____

WOULD RECOMMEND?
☐ YES   ☐ NO   ☐ MAYBE
RECOMMEND TO
_____

WOULD READ AGAIN?
☐ YES   ☐ NO   ☐ MAYBE

WOULD READ OTHER AUTHOR'S WORKS?
☐ YES   ☐ NO   ☐ MAYBE

SERIES RATING
EASE OF READING
☆☆☆☆☆
CHARACTERS
☆☆☆☆☆
PLOT
☆☆☆☆☆
ENJOYABILITY
☆☆☆☆☆

OVERALL RATING
☆☆☆☆☆

NOTES

NOTES

NOTES

NOTES

NOTES

NOTES

NOTES

NOTES

www.ingramcontent.com/pod-product-compliance
Lightning Source LLC
Chambersburg PA
CBHW061735020426
42331CB00006B/1250